Star Quality

Star Quality

Screen Actors from the Golden Age of Films

Arthur F. McClure
and
Ken D. Jones

South Brunswick and New York: A. S. Barnes and Company
London: Thomas Yoseloff Ltd

A. S. Barnes and Co., Inc.
Cranbury, New Jersey 08512

Thomas Yoseloff Ltd
108 New Bond Street
London W1Y OQX, England

Library of Congress Cataloging in Publication Data

McClure, Arthur F.
     Star quality.

     1. Moving-picture actors and actresses—United
States—Biography. I. Jones, Ken D., joint author.
II. Title.
PN1998.A2M253   791.43′028′0922 ₁B₁   73-2770
ISBN 0-498-01374-X

PRINTED IN THE UNITED STATES OF AMERICA

To Judy and Nancy . . . . . .
who also possess STAR QUALITY!

Contents

Preface

Our purpose in this book is to present a brief glimpse of a large number of movie stars of the sound era. These actors and actresses in many cases represent those who have been somewhat overlooked by film historians. In most instances they were more than featured players but not "superstars" in the present usage. It is our hope that this book will contribute to filling that historical gap left by film historians. Our intention is to provide some further understanding of that elusive phrase "star quality." It is probably impossible to write anything like a definitive history of such intangibles as movie stars, but it is possible to look back on their careers and perhaps make some sense of the impact on our lives.

The errors of omission ought to be more numerous than those of commission, but in any case the responsibility is ours.

Before closing, we should like to express our gratitude to Mss. Marsha Bird and Bonnie Schroder who were eminently cooperative and left few pages of the manuscript unimproved.

Introduction

This book appraises the movie star in American life since 1930 from a very special point of view. The authors believe that the stars have an impact far beyond the recent events of topical interest at any particular time. Thirty or forty years after films were made, they are still being shown repeatedly on television and in theaters and schools. In addition, there are social forces in American society that have caused us to celebrate the movie star on a level with royalty. The stars are a part of the escape and innocence of movies and the public's thirst for information concerning their lives is insatiable.

Star Quality is a book of memories. Any treatise on movie stars of the 1930s through the 1950s must by necessity come from the remembrances of a thousand Saturdays spent in the cool darkness of a theater—as audiences watched their fantasies take shape on the screen. *Star Quality* is a discussion of the screen personalities who peopled those fantasies. Many questions can be asked about them. Where did all of these people come from? What motivated them to come to Hollywood? Are there common characteristics among the stars? What is "star quality"? Can it be defined or can it be explained only as a part of the magic of movies?

The star system was the foundation of Hollywood's success and despite some prophets of doom, it remains so. The motion picture public still wants stars with whom they can identify, but the system has changed a great deal. The collapse of the studio star system, most experts agree, is the direct result of the economic collapse of the studios.

In the golden days of the 1930s and 1940s studios signed young performers and groomed them for years, slowly and carefully. The studio would put the youngsters in bit parts first and guide them, on and off the screen. Gradually, bigger and better parts would come. Countless times young beauty-contest winners came to Hollywood hoping for stardom, some even half expected it. They settled in and waited for the big break—if it ever came. And when they did make it big there were millions of viewers in all parts of the country to examine their presence. The movie stars were something to believe in through depression, war, and even the uncomfortable and disturbing affluence of post-war America. Hollywood glamour was a comforting escape when moviegoing was a national habit. Television, the supposed destroyer of that habit, later reinforced the phenomenon of star watching with its "late show."

The movies were simply entertaining in those days. Messages were few. For years movie fans yearned for escape and the stars provided it. The heroes were superhuman and the beautiful women had an unattainable quality. For example, there was a time when movie fans latched on to a love team in picture after picture: Jeanette MacDonald and Nelson Eddy, Fred Astaire and Ginger Rogers, Clark Gable and Joan Crawford, William Powell and Myrna Loy. Fidelity to these teams was the watchword of audiences. Screen romances are all free-lance these days and stars have a romantic interest with different partners in each picture. Veteran film fans find all this rather disturbing, and hark back to a time of perennial screen romantic teams.

Each moviegoer reacts to the expectations of a culture in his own way. Many movie historians have fallen prey to the easy generalization that the individual moviegoer is a completely passive agent, a helpless and supine pawn in an all-embracing cultural interaction between star and audience. The individual reactions ordinarily do not differ appreciably, but the important consideration is that they *do differ*. Some observers both young and old treat such endeavors as the whim of nostalgia. Many use nostalgia as a spoof of the "Establishment" by flaunting things of the past. But those who are more serious about the value of the past maintain that there is comfort that can be derived from the memories of the screen accomplishments and attributes of these people who have "star quality."

The names of stars on movie marquees with their high degree of audience identification always meant box-office receipts. One of the fascinating quests for movie historians has been to trace the careers of the "movie star" and to investigate what happened to them after their careers ended. Many came to a tragic end. Others left the acting profession to lead lives far from the glamour of Hollywood. Still others simply disappeared from public view and preferred to remain anonymous. Occasionally they made the news again only in death. During one week in May 1970, Inger Stevens, Anita Louise, Gypsy Rose Lee, and Ed Begley all died. Rarely in one week has show business suffered such a succession of losses. Each represented a differing fate, and each of their lives had a fascination for others to ponder.

Patricia Ellis and Inger Stevens represent an interesting study in contrasts. Much has been written about the destructive side of Hollywood's influence upon the lives of its stars. The lives of Patricia Ellis, a Warner Brothers star during the 1930s, and Inger Stevens, the svelte blue-eyed blonde of the 1950s and 1960s are good examples of these contrasts. Miss Stevens began her busy and unhappy career in Kansas City, and Miss Ellis lived a quietly happy married life in that city after her film career ended. This coincidental fact is perhaps the only similarity in their lives.

These two women had some things in common as movie stars, but their private lives could not have been more different. Patricia Ellis, who as a housewife often jokingly referred to herself as "Queen of the 'B' pictures for Warner Brothers," never acted after her marriage in 1941 to George T. O'Maley, a Kansas Citian who met her when she was acting in *Louisiana Purchase* on Broadway. She was born Patricia Gene O'Brien in Birmingham, Michigan, a suburb of Detroit on May 20, 1916, the daughter of Mr. and Mrs. E. G. O'Brien. At an early age she came under the tutelage of Alexander Leftwich, a New York director, who married her mother after her parents

were divorced. At nine she read every script submitted to Leftwich. At the age of twelve she was Leftwich's assistant director. In Boston, she recited from memory the lines for the entire cast of *Strike Up the Band* as Leftwich and technicians went through light changes. Leftwich had dismissed the entire cast during a dispute. After several years of stage experience, the tall blonde girl arrived in Hollywood in 1932 after a Warner Brothers screen test. She was named a "Wampas Baby Star," a promotional ploy used by Hollywood from 1922 to 1934 which generated nearly as much excitement as the Academy Awards. Such "baby stars" were tabbed by publicity men to become the stars of the future. As a Warner contract player she eventually appeared in more than forty films from 1932 to 1941.

She was the perpetual ingenue and appeared with George Arliss and Dick Powell in *The King's Vacation*, with James Cagney in *Picture Snatcher* and *St. Louis Kid*, with Joe E. Brown in *Elmer the Great*, with Douglas Fairbanks, Jr. in *The Narrow Corner*, with William Gargan in *A Night at the Ritz*, with Arthur Treacher in *Step Lively Jeeves!*, and with James Melton in *Melody for Two*. In 1941, she met her husband, George T. O'Maley, a Kansas City businessman while she was playing in *Louisiana Purchase* on Broadway, and they were married in Bowling Green, Ohio. She never appeared professionally after that.

Instead, she turned to the quiet life of Kansas City housewife and mother of a daughter, Molly. Miss Ellis always maintained that she enjoyed the latter role as fully as her acting career. She became an inveterate worker in various charities including the Easter Seal Crippled Children Society. She also taught sewing and handicrafts and was locally renowned for her dress designing. Her charity work was done with no fanfare and was achieved with a quiet dignity. On March 26, 1970, she died from cancer after a lengthy illness. Her daughter recently wrote that her mother, "was a humble and introspective woman, never wanting publicity or seeking it . . . she was no 'do-gooder' . . . merely a warm and creative woman who wanted to contribute to those around her—quietly."

There was, however, nothing quiet about the life of Inger Stevens. And she was dogged by bad luck to an almost incredible extent. Inger Stevens was born on October 18, 1934, in Stockholm, Sweden. When Miss Stevens was thirteen, she and her brother, Carl, came to the United States to live with their father, Per G. Stensland, following

Patricia Ellis with Dennis Moore in Down the Stretch
(First National, 1936).

the breakup of his marriage. At the time, Stensland was studying on a Fulbright scholarship at Harvard, but he later remarried and moved to Kansas when he was named associate professor in the Institute of Citizenship at Kansas State University, Manhattan, Kansas, in 1948 and remained on the faculty until 1951. She attended Manhattan High School and had parts in several high school plays. Unhappy there, she ran away to Kansas City at sixteen, and worked as a waitress and then as a $60-a-week dancer in a burlesque show. Her irate father came to Kansas City and took her home, but one week after she graduated from Manhattan High School she ran away again to New York, where she met Anthony Soglio, an agent who put her under contract and changed her last name to Stevens. They were married on July 9, 1955, in Greenwich, Connecticut, but separated after four months, and in 1958 they were divorced. While working in television commercials

and as a chorus girl at the Latin Quarter, Miss Stevens took acting lessons from Lee Strasberg at the Actors Studio. Soon she was seen on such prestigious television series as "Studio One," "Kraft Theater," and "Playhouse 90" in the mid-1950s.

She also appeared in New England stock company productions of *The Women* and *Glad Tidings* and made her Broadway stage debut in *Debut* in 1957, a play that closed quickly. In 1957 she was called to Hollywood by a producer who had seen her on television. In her first film, *Man on Fire,* she co-starred with widower Bing Crosby, with whom she had a highly publicized and ultimately disappointing romance. He later married Kathryn Grant. Several years later Miss Stevens became involved with another married star, a romance that also was hurtful to her. In June, 1958, she took a boat trip to Europe to rest and upon her return to the United States, went into analysis.

Inger Stevens with George Segal in **The New Interns**
(Columbia, 1964).

She felt that hard luck had always plagued her emotional life as well as her career. Although a very busy actress, there were many disquieting and tragic occurrences. She collapsed, with eleven others during the filming of *Cry Terror* in the Hudson Tubes, suffering from carbon monoxide poisoning. Her jaw was dislocated while filming a segment for "Zane Grey Theater." On New Year's Day, 1959, after a depressing New Year's Eve party, she attempted suicide. In 1961, she was the last passenger to leave a jet that crashed on landing at Lisbon and exploded seconds after her exit.

In 1963 she replaced Barbara Bel Geddes as the star of the Broadway play *Mary, Mary.* That same year she began a three-year stint on television as star of the highly successful ABC series "The Farmer's Daughter." Before the shooting began on the series, Miss Stevens collapsed under the combined pressures of overwork, underweight and

internal hemorrhaging. After quitting the television series, she became that rarity, an actress who was able to sustain a successful career as a star in films. Despite her successes, she was in her own words, "very much a hard-luck girl." In recent years she kept busy making films and also took an active interest in the problems of retarded children. Governor Pat Brown of California appointed her a member of the advisory board of the Neuropsychiatric Institute of the UCLA Medical Center. She became chairman of the California Council for Mentally Retarded Children. She also organized and sponsored a celebrity art exhibit to raise funds for the benefit of retarded children.

On April 30, 1970, Inger Stevens was found on the kitchen floor of her Hollywood home by her secretary and died in an ambulance on the way to a hospital. Her death was ruled a suicide by the coroner. Death was caused by acute intoxication

14

from barbiturates, a common ingredient of sleeping pills. Miss Stevens's other films included *The World, the Flesh and the Devil, The Buccaneer, Five Card Stud, Guide for the Married Man, Firecreek, A Long Ride Home, House of Cards, The Borgia Stick, Madigan,* and *A Dream of Kings.* To describe such a life as "meteoric" strains even an old cliché. But her sadness remains in the memory.

The movies, then, and movie stars with all of their remarkable qualities, are important parts of American culture. The stars help to shape the goals, aspirations, standards, and values that moviegoers incorporate into their personalities. The stars then become parts of the moviegoer's culture. This is part of the special magic of movies. American historians must continue to investigate this interaction that is so varied and important. The movies become a mediator as important to the individual as radio, television, or newspapers. This interaction is literally between the individuals and culture, since the individual responds symbolically to the words he hears and the figures he sees. The heroine on the screen is not so much a real person as a symbol of such social values as beauty, wealth, power, prestige, and love. In addition, by recalling the movie stars of the past, students of film history can take a serious interest in the popular culture. We can make comparisons between the life styles of then and now. This is good because it teaches students something about history in a very enjoyable way.

The old star system in Hollywood has been declared dead by many observers. At the very least there has been a deep change in the system since the days when most of the actors represented in this book were most active. Perhaps stars are no longer possible because the American public no longer attends movie houses as a habit and therefore cannot sustain the sort of evolutionary recognition of a "star quality" as in earlier years. But there is a sentimental attachment to the stars in the fond memories of movie audiences everywhere.

Star Quality

1

Rebuttal for a Friend

by

Patric Knowles

Author's note: One of Hollywood's most colorful stars was Errol Flynn. He was the exemplification of the movie star in the minds of moviegoers the world over. Much has been written about both the personal and professional life of this flamboyant man. Everything that he did was newsworthy—good or bad. But through it all, his friends anguished because of what they considered to be the overblown and somewhat mistaken public image of a man who actually was not only funloving but loyal.

Patric Knowles was one such friend. In the following article he not only illuminates the Flynn charm, but he seriously discusses Errol Flynn as a decent man who was incapable of ever intentionally hurting anyone:

Errol Flynn was my friend. I liked him immensely; I was his close companion for years. He was my son's godfather. The christening mug he presented to my son bore the inscription, "What fortune were thine, Godson, had you but entered the world with a father like me." One day, I asked him what he had meant, he just looked over at my wife, Enid, and grinned his "Flynn grin"—that charming, secret grin that made the gals shiver.

I always felt so "alive" around Flynn; never a dull moment.

I read his book *My Wicked, Wicked Ways* and, while I enjoyed it very much, there were many episodes he left untouched, enough, I should imag-

ine, to fill another volume or two. Knowing Flynn, I firmly believe he wrote every word of *My Wicked, Wicked Ways* with his tongue in a position other than dead center.

He lived life as if it were a game—a game he enjoyed playing. But he was an impatient player —not to win, but to move along to the next bout.

Those, like myself, who came to know him well, fell quickly under the spell of his charm and good looks . . . the personality which, later on, prompted the saying "in like Flynn."

He also had the luck of the Irish for sure. . . .

We were on location at a place called Chico, in northern California. We were making a film called *The Adventures of Robin Hood.* Flynn played the title role while I enacted the part of Will Scarlett, one of his merry men.

It was our custom, every evening, on returning to our hotel from filming, to stop by the small airfield just outside Chico. The operator, Bill Miller, was having a tough time (pardon the joke) getting his business off the ground. At that time (1937) I think he had a Piper Cub and an old Curtis Robin powered by an O.X.5. Not much to start a flying school with.

I had a total of fifty hours and Flynn had none —solo time, I mean. Well, I talked him into learning how to fly the Cub and I'd like to mention at this point that it took 12 hours of dual instruction to solo. Flynn made it in four hours. Our studio (Warner Bros.) somehow found out about our flying and we began to receive messages from various departments, warning us of the grave consequences should anything happen to us. One note to me asked if I realized that I was endangering the life of the star of the picture and jeopardizing the investment of several millions of dollars. No one said anything about *my* life. We ignored all the notes and messages and continued to fly each evening. Then a telegram arrived. It was addressed to me and signed by the producer of the picture. It threatened me with some sort of legal action if I persisted in encouraging Flynn to fly. (That was a private laugh in itself.)

I asked the "old boy" what we should do about the threat and he laughed loud and long, as they say. "Do you know," he said, "how many people in our business fly their own planes to and from location?"

"No, I don't," I said. "But tell me, then I can laugh, too."

"Brian Aherne, Wally Beery, Bob Taylor, Jim Stewart—just to name a few. Now don't get yourself in an uproar, old son. Just tear up the telegram and forget it." I did, then we flipped a coin to see who would fly first. He won.

"Why don't you have the driver put the car in the hangar, out of the way," he said. "Then the snoopers won't know whether we are here or not."

We hid the car in the back of the hangar while Flynn "flewed." I mean FLEWED. He phooled all over the sky, showing off. Nothing really dangerous, just hammer stalls, tight turns and wing overs. After only four hours dual he was a veritable Rickenbacker.

He didn't say a word as he climbed out of the cockpit and I got in. He simply leered at me with a let's-see-what-you-can-do look. Well, I did everything but fly through the hangar doors. Then, to finish off, climbed up to a thousand feet and did two loops, landing at the end of the second one.

You can imagine the smug grin I was wearing as I got out of the plane. I didn't wear it for long though. Two men were approaching. One man I knew; he was the production manager from the studio, the other was a stranger to me.

I'll wind it up fast for you now. The stranger was a Civil Aeronautics man. They had arrived on the field just as I had taken off and had witnessed my performance. The studio manager informed me that they were going to lodge a complaint with the Screen Actors Guild. The C.A.A. man took away my license pending the outcome of the hearing on my case at a later date. The charges? Flying in a manner to endanger the lives and property of the public. Stunting without a parachute.

Later, in the car, on the way to our hotel, I asked Flynn where he was during the excitement.

"Why, in the car having forty winks, old son," he said. "I started to learn my lines for tomorrow and simply dozed off."

That's the sort of thing I mean when I say Flynn had the luck of the Irish. By the way, the Screen Actors Guild fined me one hundred dollars and my license was re-instated at the hearing by the C.A.A. This article is entitled "Rebuttal for a Friend," but if you think I'm going to say Flynn was a virgin; never swore, or drank booze—you're mistaken. (They don't hardly make any of them anymore.) What I am going to say is this . . . Flynn never did anything vicious or hurtful to anyone in his entire life. There are some who will argue the point, of course, and so, to concede the fact that, indirectly, some people's lives were changed by Flynn's actions, I will add the word "knowingly." Flynn was a motion picture star in the true sense. A fine physique, good looks and great charm. His studio spent millions of dollars publicizing his movies and, as a result, Flynn, too. The publicity department received instructions to "go-all-out" on him after his first success. They did just that and they created a Flynn who simply didn't exist—until much later.

Flynn and I were under contract to Warner Bros. in England. Irving Asher, the head of the studio, was the one who sent Flynn to Hollywood and so, I would say, discovered Flynn. Anyway, when they were casting *The Charge of the Light Brigade* in Hollywood, they discovered they had no one to play the part of Flynn's brother. Irving Asher sent Jack Warner some film of mine and I was approved for the part.

Flynn and I renewed our acquaintance on location at Lone Pine, California, and became fast friends while making The Charge.

Thirty-five years ago, Flynn and I were supposed to look alike. Neither of us could see it though. Someone started the rumor that I had been brought to Hollywood strictly as a "threat" to Flynn. He had risen to the heights so quickly, they expected trouble from him and I was the studio's "pinch hitter."

I first heard of the rumor when a nationally syndicated columnist called me for an interview. I was quite inexperienced in the ways of answering questions in those days and the resulting statements I was supposed to have uttered were printed in all the newspapers in the country. I was embarrassed to say the least, but the "old boy" called me to

Rosalind Russell, Errol Flynn, Olivia De Havilland, and Patric Knowles in Four's a Crowd *(Warner Bros., 1938).*

say he liked the interview and I should always "keep it interesting" in future publicity.

Flynn knew he had no worries about my taking over from him. In the first place, in nightclubs I'm a coward, but a live coward. I have enough trouble fighting the booze, never mind the customers. In the second place, "in like Knowles" doesn't rhyme.

I visited him on the set a few months before he passed away. We talked of the old days and when I left he put his arm around my shoulder and said with a grin, "Let me know, old son, when you want to take over. I'm getting too old for this sort of thing." I knew him when he wasn't too old for anything. Like the time we were in Balboa, California . . .

Flynn, myself, and three or four cronies were spending a weekend on his yacht *Sirocco*. We left the boat moored in the channel and went ashore to stretch our legs and visit one of the many pubs. All of us were fairly well known in the movies and word soon spread around that we

were in Balboa at a certain tavern. Five or six teen-age girls entered the place and demanded our autographs. We obliged them and invited them to have a soft drink.

Well, you know how things are. We sat around talking to the girls for half an hour, then they left. Soon after, we departed. We intended to return to the boat and take a swim. But on the dock, waiting for us, were half a dozen of the biggest teen-age football stars I ever want to see. As I mentioned before, I'm a live coward and a couple of the other blokes weren't at all shy about retiring either. We ignored the small boat waiting to transport us back to the big boat and dove into the bay fully clothed. As we swam out we could hear Flynn whooping away on the dock. Looking back, Flynn was holding off the enemy and laughing while doing it. He was *enjoying* himself.

The kids finally drove him off the dock by sheer weight of numbers. He swam to the boat and as we dragged him aboard he gasped, "Friends of the gals in the pub."

You know how that little episode appeared in the papers? "FLYNN IN BRAWL OVER GIRL."

Many times, while in Flynn's company, I have seen some noble and brave types, full of "flit" usually, walk up to him and open with, "You're not so G..D...tough. I could take you with one arm behind my back." He'd say it in a loud voice then turn around and shout to someone across the room, "See honey. I did it." Then, encouraged by his success, he would press his luck further. Flynn would try to be patient, he'd "yes" the guy and sometimes buy him a drink. He often was forced to leave the premises.

Flynn was a great organizer, too. . . .

The scene: on location, somewhere in northern California, the film we were making, *Robin Hood*.

We were relaxing in his dressing trailer between shooting scenes. "Flynn," I said, "my mother and father-in-law arrive from England tomorrow evening. They plan to stay here at the hotel with us for a week." Flynn looked up from the book he was reading with a startled expression.

"What did you say, old son? In-laws. That's earth-shattering. Is there no way to stall them?"

"None whatever," I replied. "They're flying up from Los Angeles and will be here at six."

Flynn sighed, "Well, if it's inevitable, relax and enjoy it. But my heart bleeds for you."

"Now wait a minute," I said. "These people are nice—for in-laws, that is. I'm sure you'll like them."

"Where in-laws are concerned, I concur with the general opinion; generally speaking, that is."

"My problem is . . . what do I do with them to keep them amused?"

"You can invite them out to the location to watch us shoot the picture. And think, they may have the dubious honor of eating a box lunch with us." Flynn returned to his book.

"These people have seen dozens of pictures being made," I said. "No, I mean something big. Something out of the ordinary, something that will let them know how much I respect them. Don't forget, they let me marry their daughter, Enid."

Flynn lowered the book and gave me his "jaundiced-eye" look. (He was quite fond of Enid, I guess.) He concentrated for a moment, then said, "I think I have an idea, old son."

"Let me know when you are sure," I said.

He thought for a moment longer. "There are roughly two hundred people here on location. Fifty of those people are in the entertainment business. There are dancers, jugglers, singers and stunt men."

"No actors?" I asked, while looking him in the eye.

He gave me the "lifted-eyebrow" look. "We have Eugene Pallette," he said.

"Fine actor," I agreed. "But what has all this to do with my in-laws?"

"A banquet, chum."

"A banquet?"

"Yes. We can call it a rehearsal for the scene we are going to do in the picture later. We'll have it at the hotel and Gene Pallette will be in charge of the grub. He's one of the finest cooks I know and I'm sure he'll be only too glad to help. That ought to give your people the right impression."

At the hotel later that evening we put it up to Gene and he was delighted. He said he would take charge of the kitchen on one condition though . . . that he would have complete control over the menu; no interference at all from anyone. I happily agreed. The next morning, on location, we received a message from Gene to the effect that the main course was to be suckling pig and he would need three of them; also, it was up to us to produce them. We made inquiries and found a slaughterhouse in the neighborhood. Through them, we found the name and address of a pig farmer. Howard Hill, the world-famous archer, suggested we ride over and talk to the farmer. Now "cut" to the pig farm and try to imagine the farmer going about his chores. He hears the thudding sound of horses hooves in the distance. He looks up and sees three horses bearing down upon him, carrying on their backs three men dressed in the traditional apparel of the Robin Hood era. Flynn, Howard Hill, and myself clothed in tights, jerkins and caps with a trailing feather on top. Armed to the teeth with swords, bows and arrows.

The farmer couldn't have been any more startled if a flying saucer had landed beside him. He took off at a dead run for his farmhouse with the three of us following close behind.

It took us twenty minutes to convince the man that we were not mad, going to kill him, and what we wanted. Once he made up his mind we were on the level he was with us one hundred per cent. He entered into the spirit of the things, and helped us select the three best young pigs from his large herd. (Or is it flock?) We paid him and with a salute to the farmer, Robin and two of his merry men rode off into the distance, each clutching a squealing pig under his arm.

There's more.

The slaughterhouse people must have heard we were on our way because the place was locked up tight and not a soul could we find. Howard suggested we ride back to location and start from there. He also offered to slaughter the pigs and dress them if we were stuck. Sooo—off rode Robin and two not so merry men into the distance, each fighting a heavy little pig.

Arriving back at the location we found the crew had wrapped up for the day and gone back to the hotel. It was getting dark now. There was no transportation to be had anywhere.

Soooo—off rode Robin and two mad as hell merry men into the distance, each carrying under his arm a lousy little pig that seemed to weigh a ton and to be dipped in grease.

The hotel was there still. The in-laws were there, too. Gene Pallette was waiting for his pigs. The banquet was ready to begin. We were two hours late. Somehow, during the greetings and the relating of our sad story, the three lousy little bastard pigs got away. They were heard squealing with laughter in the woods nearby as we later sat down to a banquet of hamburgers. (But delicious, Gene, wherever you are.)

Flynn was generous to a fault and sometimes it annoyed me to see the way he was taken—even by close friends.

I almost took him for a hundred and sixty dollars once. . . .

I was in Canada, with the RCAF as a flying instructor. I had some leave coming so, like a flash, I headed for Hollywood. I caught up with Flynn at the Hotel del Coronado in San Diego. He was making a picture. After hinting to him he invited me to visit him for a few days and, since he had a suite, said I could stay with him. He worked all day and retired early to study his script for the next day's work. As a result, I didn't have much time with him. I was left to myself and, well, I spent all my money amusing myself. I was broke—not even enough to pay my fare back to the Canadian border. I mentioned the fact to Flynn.

I wrote to him later and thanked him for his generosity. I quote the letter he wrote me in reply.

Hotel del Coronado

My Patric Knowles
R.C.A.F.
C/O Hotel Saskachewan
Regina, Saskatchewan, Canada.
My dear old bastard:
Thanks for your letter. I don't mind you going to see my business manager. I don't mind you getting into him, or rather me, for one hundred and sixty clams—I don't mind a lot of other things about you, but I do wish when next you come to stay with me you will not use all the towels in my bathroom, depriving me of any means to dry my glorious body, apart from the curtains. In short, you can go too far. This is particularly embarrassing when some little beauty with whom I am slightly acquainted and trying to impress, goes into the bathroom and has to wind up using the bath mat with which to dry her pretty, little face. What did you do with the towels? Are things that bad in Canada?

Old son, it was wonderful to see you, but particularly annoying not to have the least chance for one of those long gossips—philosophical, lude, erudite, charming, nonsensical, and all the rest of the dribble we had sometimes spent a few hours drooling over. I did so want to talk to you, but you were stewed and I was busy working. Don't worry about the dough. Forget it. It doesn't bother me in the least, except that I hope it was enough to see you back to that drear spot in Canada.

I do hope, son, that you don't go overseas. I know you are depressed and can readily understand why, but, chum, don't, for Christ's sake, do anything as dumb as that. Stick it out for a while longer. Perhaps you can wangle a little more time later. If you know that you can get a few weeks, let me know a little beforehand, and I promise I will go out as your agent and hunt you a job myself.

So long, chum, and drop me a swift line.   Errol.

As a footnote to the above, it was five years before I was able to repay Flynn the one hundred and sixty clams.

Flynn's passing and the subsequent attacks on his way of life started me thinking. Didn't someone once say something about, "he who casts the first stone?" Then there was another saying about how one should tidy up one's own house first. Who are we to judge our fellow man? Was Flynn right or wrong in his way of life? I thought about it a great deal, and as a result was inspired to write a novel. (My first, entitled *Even Steven*, in which the central character lives his life much the same way as Flynn lived his.)

It was his life. He lived the way he wanted to—as an individual. And, in these days of high taxation; fear of being wiped off the face of the earth at any moment, I, for one, wish that before they nail the coffin lid down on me I had—well, don't you?

Patric Knowles

2
Biographies

Don Ameche (1908–   )

Don Ameche was born Dominic Felix Amici on May 31, 1908, in Kenosha, Wisconsin. He was one of eight children born to Felix and Barbara Amici. His elementary school days were spent in Kenosha and he spent four years at Columbia Academy in Dubuque, Iowa. He also attended Columbia College in the same city. It was there that he met his wife, Honore Prendergast.

His father wanted him to become a lawyer, and in pursuit of this career he entered Georgetown University in Washington, D.C. He later changed to the University of Wisconsin in Madison. It was there that he became interested in acting and participated in the college plays. He also participated in plays put on by the local stock companies.

Leaving his law career for acting, he left Madison for New York City. In 1929 he appeared in a show called *Jerry For Short*. He then joined Texas Guinan in a vaudeville show touring the U.S.A. He later auditioned for a part on radio in "The Empire Builder" and this started a long and successful association with the popular forerunner to television.

On radio he played Bob Drake on "Betty and Bob," John Bickerson on "The Bickersons," Pasquale on "The Edgar Bergen and Charlie McCarthy Show," Captain Hughes on "Jack Armstrong, the All-American Boy," and had featured roles in "Milligan and Mulligan," "The National Farm and Home Hour," "The Jimmy Durante Show," "Grand Hotel," and "The First Nighter."

His popularity in this medium led to his film career and he was signed to a contract by 20th Century-Fox after being rebuffed by MGM. His first screen role was a dual one in *Sins of Man* in 1936 with Jean Hersholt. He appeared in many notable films for Fox including *Ramona, In Old Chicago, Alexander's Ragtime Band, The Story of Alexander Graham Bell, Swanee River, Lillian Russell, Four Sons, That Night in Rio, Moon Over Miami, Heaven Can Wait,* and *Wing and a Prayer.*

His rich baritone singing and speaking voice and pleasant personality carried over into television with further success. He still appears in an occasional movie.

Don Ameche with Andrea Leeds in Swanee River
(20th Century-Fox, 1939).

Evelyn Ankers (1918–   )

Evelyn Ankers was born August 17, 1918, in Valparaiso, Chile, of English parents. Her father was a mining engineer. Later her family returned to England where she studied singing and dancing. In England, she was given a small part in *Belles of St. Mary's* in 1936. After this film she entered the Royal Academy of Dramatic Art for further seasoning. She made several films shown in England from 1936 through 1938.

She moved to the United States and appeared on the New York stage in 1940 in *Ladies in Retirement*. Her role as the maid in this suspense thriller gave American audiences their first opportunity to experience the Ankers "scream." When the play moved to Los Angeles she was signed to a seven-year contract by Universal. She met actor Richard Denning and they were married in 1942. She had already gained fame by appearing in several horror films and while Denning enlisted in the U.S. Navy shortly after their marriage, her career hit full stride and she soon became known as "The Queen of the Horror Films." She put her famous scream to good use in these films as she coolly played opposite Lon Chaney, Jr., Bela Lugosi, Lionel Atwill, Basil Rathbone, and George Zucco.

Her many films included *Hold That Ghost, The Wolf Man, The Ghost of Frankenstein, Captive Wild Woman, The Mad Ghoul, Son of Dracula, Weird Woman, The Frozen Ghost, The Fatal Witness, Eagle Squadron, All By Myself, Ladies Courageous, The French Key, Tarzan's Magic Fountain,* and *The Texan Meets Calamity Jane.*

She never seemed to really enjoy her film career and she made her last film in 1950 while her husband continued to appear on the screen. They are still happily married, have one daughter, and divide their time between living in California and Hawaii.

Evelyn Ankers with David Bruce and George Zucco in **The Mad Ghoul** *(Universal, 1943).*

William Bendix with Lanny Ross and Rosemary De-Camp in The Life of Riley *(Universal, 1949).*

William Bendix (1906–1964)

William Bendix had a rough, gruff manner that masked a soft heart. Bendix was that rarity, a character actor who became a star. But whereas most stars have fancy profiles and faultless physiques, he was built like a barrel and had a face like several miles of bad road. He once remarked that he was "about as handsome as a mud fence." But he was fascinating to watch. In his occasional roles as a heavy he radiated pure brute force and menace. Playing the pal of conventional heroes on numerous occasions, he was a convincing hail-fellow-well-met.

Born in New York City, January 14, 1906, he tried a variety of jobs before becoming a successful actor—bat boy for the New York Giants, semiprofessional baseball player, singing waiter, grocer. Bendix had a brief stint on the boards at 16 as a member of the Henry Street Settlement House Players. But not until he joined the Federal theater project in the mid-1930s did he make acting a career—despite a string of six flops on Broadway. His first hit was as a policeman in William Saroyan's *The Time of Your Life* in

1939. He went to Hollywood in 1941 to appear in *Woman of the Year.* The obvious sincerity beneath his rough-hewn exterior made him a convincing performer. Soon he was starring on his own, notably in Eugene O'Neill's *The Hairy Ape.* Bendix appeared in about fifty films, among them *Wake Island, Guadalcanal Diary, Lifeboat, Babe Ruth Story, Hostages, Two Years Before The Mast, A Connecticut Yankee, Detective Story, Crashout,* and his last one, *Invitation To A Hanging.*

It was in low comedy that he found his widest audience and financial independence in radio, television, and films. Starting as a radio series in January, 1944, and running for eight seasons before moving to television in January, 1953, Bendix starred in "The Life of Riley" as Chester A. Riley. He later appeared in a western television series "Overland Stage." He returned to the Broadway theater in 1960 replacing Jackie Gleason in the musical *Take Me Along.* On December 14, 1964, he died of lumbar pneumonia in Los Angeles.

27

Charles Bickford with Cary Grant in Mr. Lucky *(RKO, 1943).*

Charles Bickford (1890–1967)

Charles Bickford was known to movie audiences for his portrayals of industrialists, fathers, and politicians. He was, however, proud of his private image of nonconformist. His associates described him as hard, strong and gruff, yet very fair-minded. His crinkled hair and granite features were his trademarks in his films.

Born on New Year's Day, 1890, in Cambridge, Massachusetts, Bickford got his first job in show business in burlesque in San Francisco. He then joined a Boston stock company to gain dramatic experience and twelve years later made his debut on Broadway in Maxwell Anderson's *Outside Looking In.* He made his screen debut in *Dynamite* in 1929 with C. B. DeMille producing his first talking picture for MGM. During a disagreement, the hot-tempered Bickford struck the director and knocked him down. Instead of his career being finished the two men became close friends. His speak-your-mind attitude was the basis of another famous dispute with Louis B. Mayer, who fired him with the promise that he would never again work in films.

Bickford first attracted serious attention as a film actor with his second picture opposite Greta Garbo in MGM's *Anna Christie* in 1930. He went on to become one of the most respected actors in motion pictures. His acting prowess was recognized in his being nominated three times for Academy Awards for supporting roles in *Johnny Belinda, The Farmer's Daughter,* and *Song of Bernadette.* Among his other best-known pictures were *Little Miss Marker, East of Java, Pride of the Marines, Reap the Wild Wind, Wing and a Prayer, Duel in the Sun, Command Decision, A Star Is Born, Not as a Stranger, The Court-Martial of Billy Mitchell, The Big Country, The Unforgiven,* and *Days of Wine and Roses.*

In 1965 he replaced Lee J. Cobb as the owner of Shiloh Ranch in "The Virginian" television series. In the same year he published his autobiography, *Bulls, Balls, Bicycles and Actors.* On November 9, 1967, he died in Los Angeles from an earlier attack of emphysema later complicated by attacks of pneumonia and a bloodstream infection.

Joan Blondell (1909–   )

During the 1930s and 1940s Joan Blondell spent most of her time in movies as everybody's slightly dizzy Broadway blonde. She was born on August 30, 1909, in New York City, the daughter of actor Eddie Blondell, the original "Katzenjammer Kid." Miss Blondell has been on the stage since childhood where she toured Europe, China, and Australia with the family vaudeville act. She did her first dramatic work with a stock company in Dallas, Texas, and was on the New York stage in *Tarnish, The Trial of Mary Dugan,* and *Ziegfeld Follies.* She began her career in movies after appearing with James Cagney in *Penny Arcade.* They both became very popular stars for Warner Brothers for many years. In 1930, she and Cagney both appeared in the Warner's version of *Penny Arcade,* which was changed to *Sinners' Holiday.* From then on it was Joan Blondell and James Cagney in many pictures including *Public Enemy, Blonde Crazy,* and *Other Men's Women.*

She appeared with many leading men such as Humphrey Bogart, Edward G. Robinson, Leslie Howard, Bing Crosby, John Wayne, and Clark Gable. In all she has appeared in nearly a hundred films during her career. Among her other films are *Three On a Match, East Side of Heaven, Two Girls on Broadway, Model Wife, Lady for a Night, Christmas Eve, The Blue Veil,* and probably her best, *A Tree Grows in Brooklyn.* Still a working actress, she has been a busy character actress in recent years with roles in *Angel Baby, The Cincinnati Kid, Mother Superior,* and many others. She had made scores of television and stage appearances and in 1968 became a regular on television's "Here Come the Brides" series. She won an Oscar nomination in 1951 for her role as the faded nightclub singer in *The Blue Veil.*

Miss Blondell was recently quoted as attributing her longevity to her screen quality that, "reminded secretaries, waitresses, reporters, chorus girls and now fading anybodies that a girl who didn't get the best of everything could eventually reach some of the goals in life."

Joan Blondell in Topper Returns *(United Artists, 1941).*

Johnny Mack Brown (1904–   )

Johnny Mack Brown was born one of nine children September 1, 1904, in Dothan, Alabama. He entered the University of Alabama in 1924 where he participated in college plays. More important he also was elected to the All-American Football team of 1927. As a halfback he was an excellent field runner and pass receiver. On New Year's Day in the 1926 Rose Bowl his underdog Alabama team defeated the University of Washington 20-19 on the strength of Johnny's catching two touchdown passes, in the waning moments of the game.

He became acquainted with actor George Fawcett on a film location in Alabama. Fawcett urged the young football player to try films. When Alabama returned to the Rose Bowl to play Stanford in 1927 Johnny came as the assistant coach. He looked up Fawcett, who showed him around the studios. A contract with MGM followed and shortly thereafter he had a bit role in *Slide, Kelly, Slide*. Other bit roles followed including that of a cavalry officer opposite Jackie Coogan in *The Bugle Call*. Later that year he made his debut as a leading man in *The Fair Co-ed* opposite Marion Davies. His career really blossomed as he worked opposite some of the great ladies of the screen including Greta Garbo, Norma Shearer, Mary Pickford, and Joan Crawford.

In 1930, King Vidor directed Johnny in a screen classic, *Billy the Kid*, where he had the title role and Wallace Beery was Pat Garrett. The film changed his image for the years ahead even though he did play in several non-westerns the remainder of his film career. In 1935 his western career got into full swing when he made a series of films for Supreme. This was followed by several for Republic studios. He also appeared in several serials, *Fighting with Kit Carson* for Mascot and *Rustlers of Red Dog, Wild West Days, Flaming Frontiers,* and *The Oregon Trail* for Universal. In 1939 he made a series of westerns for Universal that were among the best ever produced. He was supported by Bob Baker in the first few and Tex Ritter in the rest. Fuzzy Knight was the comic sidekick. His starring western roles were completed when he appeared in Monogram films for the next several years ending in 1952. With the exception of a bit role in a 1953 western he retired from the screen. He did appear on television in such shows as "Perry Mason" and "Tales of Wells Fargo." In 1961 he became the host-manager of the Tail o' the Cock restaurant in Beverly Hills. In 1965 he appeared in two Alex Gordon westerns that featured a large cast of former western players, and in 1966 played a villain in *Apache Uprising*.

In 1926 he married his college sweetheart, Cornelia Foster, and they had three daughters and a son. His storybook life as a football hero and movie star was enriched even further as he was elected to the Football Hall of Fame. Some of his other films were *Our Dancing Daughters, The Single Standard, Coquette, Every Man's Law, The Secret Six, Belle of the Nineties, Wells Fargo, Born to the West, West of Carson City, Son of Roaring Dan, Ragtime Cowboy Joe, Ride 'Em Cowboy!, The Boss of Hangtown, The Old Chisholm Trail, The Navajo Trail, Under Arizona Skies, Over the Border,* and *Texas City*.

Johnny Mack Brown in Canyon Ambush *(Monogram, 1952).*

Bruce Cabot with Marion Martin in Sinners in Paradise *(Universal, 1938).*

Bruce Cabot (1904–1972)

Bruce Cabot was born Jacques Etienne de Bujac in Carlsbad, New Mexico, on April 20, 1904. His grandfather had been the French ambassador to the United States. He attended the University of the South and became a cowboy, oil field worker, and boxer before deciding upon an acting career.

In 1932 he made his debut as a villain in *Roadhouse Murder*. The following year he was chosen to play the hero Jack Driscoll who saved Fay Wray from the clutches of the big ape in the classic film, *King Kong*. This enabled him to star as a cowboy, tough guy, or soldier of fortune in many films although many were very undistinguished films.

His exploits off the screen were as colorful as his movie roles as he hobnobbed with King Farouk of Egypt, skylarked with Errol Flynn and his cronies, and was a fixture at the health and gambling spas of Europe.

During World War II he served in the Air Force in Africa, Italy, and Sicily and resumed his career upon his return. He also had his name

legally changed to Bruce Cabot as he contended his real name constituted a professional liability; people could not remember it.

His films included *Ann Vickers, Murder on the Blackboard, Show Them No Mercy, The Last of the Mohicans, Bad Man of Brimstone, Dodge City, Susan and God, Wild Bill Hickok Rides, Fancy Pants*, and *Cat Ballou*. He later became a very close friend of John Wayne who found character roles for Cabot in many of his films including *The Comancheros, Hatari!, McLintock!, In Harm's Way, The War Wagon, The Green Berets, Hellfighters, The Undefeated, Chisum*, and *Big Jake*.

He was married three times to actresses Adrienne Ames, Grace Mary Mather Smith, and Franchesca de Scaffa. He underwent radiation treatment for lung cancer at Loma Linda University Medical Center in 1971 and was discharged in "satisfactory condition." He died of this disease at the Motion Picture Country Home and Hospital on May 3, 1972.

Judy Canova (1916–   )

Judy Canova's hillbilly image in films made her a favorite with audiences in the 1940s and 1950s. Born in Jacksonville, Florida, on November 20, 1916, she became a part of a family vaudeville act until 1934. In 1935 she went to Hollywood and her first role was in *Going Highbrow* for Warner's. Director Busby Berkeley hired her for her second film, *In Caliente*, a singing part without billing. In the picture she butchered a song called "The Lady in Red" and was an instant hit. Many roles followed including *Scatterbrain, Puddin'*

Head, Joan of Ozark, Louisiana Hayride, Hit the Hay, and *Singin' in the Corn.*

She branched out into radio and had a very popular half-hour show during the World War II years and on into the 1950s. She also appeared on television frequently. Her last screen appearance was in *The Adventures of Huckleberry Finn* in 1960. She is now semiretired and lives quietly as Mrs. Philip Rivero in the San Fernando Valley with her husband and two daughters.

Judy Canova with Allen Jenkins in Singin' In the Corn *(Columbia, 1946).*

John Carroll (1913–)

John Carroll was born Julian LaFaye in New Orleans, Louisiana, on July 17, 1913. Somewhere between the age of 10 and 13 he ran away to Houston, Texas, to become a newsboy. At 14, he tossed rivets in a steel mill and also tried his hand at being a steeplejack, ship's cook, dock laborer, range rider, barnstorming airman, racing driver, and merchant seaman.

He returned to New Orleans and completed his education and studied voice. He managed to make it to Europe where he sang in Paris, London, Berlin, Vienna, Rome, and Budapest. He appeared in such shows as *Marion, Devil May Care, Rogue Song, Dough Boys, Hearts in Exile, New Moon,* and *Reaching For the Moon.* While in Paris he also worked as a taxi driver and deep-sea diver for extra money.

He also drifted around the world on a freighter and circled the globe several times. He stopped off in Hollywood several times and even helped to build studio sound stages. He was tested by RKO in 1935 as they were looking for an athletic singer to star in *Hi, Gaucho!.* He married his leading lady in the film, Steffi Duna. His other RKO films were *Murder On the Bridle Path, Muss 'Em up,* and *We Who Are About to Die.*

In 1937 he was hired by Republic to play the lead in the 12-chapter serial *Zorro Rides Again.* Other film roles included *Only Angels Have Wings, Wolf Call, Congo Maisie, Susan and God, Hired Wife, Go West, Lady Be Good, Rio Rita, Pierre of the Plains, Flying Tigers, Hit Parade of 1943, Bedside Manner, Fiesta, Wyoming, The Fabulous Texan, I, Jane Doe, The Avengers, Surrender, Belle Le Grande, The Farmer Takes A Wife,* and *Decision at Sundown.*

His career was interrupted by World War II and he became a lieutenant in the Army Air Force. His off-the-screen life rivaled Errol Flynn, as his escapades made the headlines several times.

John Carroll in Angel in Exile *(Republic, 1948).*

Jack Carson with Ginger Rogers in **The Groom Wore Spurs** *(Universal-International, 1951).*

Jack Carson (1910–1963)

Throughout his film career, Jack Carson was best known for his ability to play the big blusterer with a witty ability to enliven any party. Physically a large man, at six feet two and one-half inches, weighing 200 pounds, he was a master of the double take, the over-the-shoulder glance with bulging eye, wrinkling forehead, and open mouth. Carson was born on October 27, 1910, in Carmen, Manitoba, Canada, but moved as a youngster to Milwaukee.

Although Carson's career from vaudeville to movies was mostly comedy, he was a better-than-average serious actor. He etched two memorable performances in *A Star is Born* and *Cat on a Hot Tin Roof*. He always considered himself an actor rather than a comedian but had difficulty breaking out of the movie mold of amusing loudmouth. In 1935 and 1936, Carson was a singing master of ceremonies at the Tower Theater in Kansas City. He had come to Kansas City as a part of a vaudeville team. It folded and he got the emcee job for a two-week run, and stayed two years. But he was determined to crack Hollywood and went there in 1937 where he broke into films. He spent many years at Warner Brothers where he described himself as their "handy man." In most films he was the character who always lost the girl.

After leaving Warner's in 1950, Carson became one of the first film stars to enter television, doing a series of one-hour comedy programs for NBC. He also had a popular radio show in which he played himself. The show also had Mel Blanc, Arthur Treacher, Elizabeth Patterson, Dave Willock, the Freddy Martin Orchestra, and Howard Petrie, announcer. Some of his movie roles included *Bringing Up Baby, Mr. Smith Goes to Washington, The Strawberry Blonde, The Male Animal, Arsenic and Old Lace, Hollywood Canteen, Roughly Speaking, Mildred Pierce, Two Guys from Milwaukee, A Star is Born, Cat on a Hot Tin Roof,* and *Rally Round The Flag, Boys!*

In his last years, Carson toured the country in stock shows. He collapsed on stage August 26, 1962, at an Andover, New Jersey, stage during a dress rehearsal of *Critic's Choice.* Six months later he died of cancer of the liver on January 2, 1963. Not long before he died he was quoted as saying, "I'm best at making people laugh, at entertainment. They don't want me for the morbid oversexed stuff Hollywood is turning out nowadays."

*Tom Conway with Erford Gage and Elaine Shepard
in* The Falcon in Danger *(RKO, 1943).*

Tom Conway (1904–1967)

Two generations of moviegoers remember Tom Conway as the suave, British-accented hero of the Falcon movie series. He was born on September 15, 1904, in St. Petersburg, Russia, of British parents. His real name was Thomas Charles Sanders. He was schooled in England and after repertory in Manchester and radio work throughout England he came to the United States to join his brother, actor George Sanders.

In 1942 he replaced his brother as detective-hero of *The Falcon* in RKO's popular film series. He played that part until the series ended in 1947. Simultaneously, he played the title roles in two popular radio series of "Sherlock Holmes" and "The Saint." In the 1950s he played the title role in the television series "Inspector Mark Sabre." After 1947 he got fewer roles and in 1953 he returned to England until 1956 where he appeared in several films. His last acting role was on the "Perry Mason" television series in the mid-1960s.

Eye trouble put an end to his employment and he became estranged from his brother.

About a year before his death he was found penniless in a $2-a-day hotel in Venice, California. He had earned as much as $4500 a week as the star of such films as *One Touch of Venus,* which launched the career of Ava Gardner. His desperate situation came to light when the manager of the hotel telephoned the Santa Monica newspaper to see if he could be helped. He was living on a federal old-age benefit. Conway spent four months in a county hospital and three months in a convalescent sanitarium for treatment of a liver ailment. He was preparing to return to work when he died on April 22, 1967. Some of his screen credits included *Sky Murder, Free and Easy, Rio Rita, The Cat People, A Night of Adventure, Lost Honeymoon, Painting the Clouds With Sunshine,* and one of the voices in *101 Dalmatians* for Walt Disney in 1961.

Larry "Buster" Crabbe (1908–   )

Larry Crabbe was born Clarence Linden Crabbe February 7, 1908, in Oakland, California. When he was quite young his family moved to Hawaii, where he became an outstanding high school athlete and an expert swimmer. He returned to the United States and entered college at the University of Southern California and upon his graduation was tested for the role of *Tarzan* by Metro in 1931. The test was of no avail.

He competed in the 1932 Olympics and was the swimming champion in the 400-meter free-style event breaking Johnny Weissmuller's 1924 record. At one time he held 5 world records and 35 national championships for swimming. After his victory in the Olympics, he was signed by Paramount. He had already appeared in *Most Dangerous Game* for RKO and *That's My Boy* for Columbia in 1932. He had the title role in Paramount's *King of the Jungle* where he played Kaspa, the Lion Man who bore a strong resemblance to Tarzan. He made his first serial, *Tarzan, the Fearless* for Principal in 1933. He was married the same year and decided to go back to the University of Southern California to study law unless he could really make it as an actor.

He became the name more closely associated with the serial hero than any other, and his role as Flash Gordon became a classic as it became the most popular of all serials even showing at first-run theaters. He appeared in the title role in *Flash Gordon, Flash Gordon's Trip to Mars,* and *Flash Gordon Conquers the Universe* and his bouts with Ming the Merciless, played by Charles Middleton, are still being shown in theaters today. He became closely associated with another comic-strip hero, Buck Rogers, in a serial by the same name for Universal in 1939. Other serials in which he starred were *Red Barry* for Universal in 1938, *The Sea Hound* in 1947 for Columbia, *Pirates of the High Seas* in 1950 for Columbia, and *King of the Congo* in 1952 for Columbia.

In the 1930s he appeared in many Zane Grey westerns for Paramount and 1941 started a string of *Billy the Kid* films for PRC with Al "Fuzzy" St. John as the comic sidekick. In the late 1940s he formed an aqua show touring the world. In 1956 he starred in *Captain Gallant of the French Foreign Legion* on television. His son, "Cuffy," co-starred and the series was very popular. He has appeared in only a few films since this series and they have all been westerns.

His time is now spent as aquatic director of the Hotel Concord in New York's Catskill mountains, supervising his swimming pool corporation, and he makes an occasional television commercial. He lives in Rye, New York, and is still married to his first wife, Adah Virginia Held after 40 years of marriage. In 1971 he went back to the Los Angeles Swim Stadium and set a world record in the 400-meter free style for the over-60 age group.

*Buster Crabbe, Richard Alexander, Frank Shannon,
and Donald Kerr in* Flash Gordon's Trip to Mars
(Universal, 1938).

Alan Curtis (1909–1953)

Alan Curtis was born Harry Ueberroth in Chicago, Illinois, on July 24, 1909. He was a taxi-cab driver in that city when his photogenic face was discovered. He was hired as a model for sports clothes and bathing suits. He went to New York and became a commercial artist's model and appeared in *Vogue*.

The handsome Curtis was given a screen test and his first role in films was that of a sailor for RKO's *Winterset* in 1936. Other films included *Between Two Women, China Passage, Mannequin, Yellow Jack, Shopworn Angel, Sgt. Madden, Four Sons, High Sierra, Come Live With Me, Remember Pearl Harbor, Gung Ho!, Hitler's Hangman, Follow the Boys, Frisco Sal, The Naughty Nineties, Flight to Nowhere, Apache Chief,* and *The Masked Pirate*.

During World War II he served in the Coast Guard. His three marriages all ended in divorce. His first was to actress Priscilla Lawson, his second was to actress Ilona Massey, and his third was to Betty Dodero.

On January 26, 1953, he underwent a kidney operation at St. Clare's Hospital in New York. A few hours after the operation he was sitting up in bed sipping tea when his heart stopped beating. A resident physician happened to enter the room and noticed his collapse. He massaged Curtis's heart by hand for four minutes before it began to beat again. He appeared to be recovering when he died on February 2, 1953.

Alan Curtis with Ella Raines in The Phantom Lady (Universal, 1944).

Joan Davis (1907–1961)

Joan Davis in Tail Spin *(20th Century-Fox, 1939).*

Joan Davis built her film career as a comedienne around outrageous gestures, hard falls, muscle-straining grimaces, and a raucous voice. She was born on June 29, 1907, in St. Paul, Minnesota, and at the age of three she began appearing as a singer and dancer before local audiences. As a child performer she toured the Pantages Theatre circuit billed as "The Toy Comedienne." Before she reached her late teens, she had performed on virtually every vaudeville circuit in the country. She married her vaudeville partner, Seremus "Si" Wills, in 1931, and "Wills and Davis" played the Palace in New York in the mid-1930s. They toured until 1936 when they went to Hollywood.

Miss Davis's first screen appearance was as a hillbilly in a Mack Sennett short *Way Up Thar* in 1934. Between 1936 and 1941 she appeared in about 25 films including *Time Out for Romance, Thin Ice, Love and Hisses, Josette, Hold That Co-ed, Sun Valley Serenade, Hold That Ghost,* and *Two Latins From Manhattan.* In 1941 she made her radio debut as a guest with Rudy Vallee, and when he joined the Coast Guard in 1943 she took over his show. Miss Davis became one of radio's most successful comediennes and in 1944 she won the *Motion Picture Daily*'s "Fame Poll." In 1945 she signed a radio contract with the United Drug Company for $1,000,000 a year for four years.

In the 1950s, Miss Davis formed her own production company, Joan Davis Productions, and made motion pictures and her television series "I Married Joan." Her other films included *Show Business, Kansas City Kitty, George White's Scandals, If You Knew Susie, Traveling Saleswoman,* and her last film, *Harem Girl.* On May 22, 1961, she died of a heart attack in Palm Springs, California.

Frances Dee with Edward Ellis and John Wayne in
A Man Betrayed *(Republic, 1941).*

Frances Dee (1907–   )

Frances Dee was born November 26, 1907, in Los Angeles, California. After graduation from Hyde Park High School in Chicago she studied at the University of Chicago for two years. She wasn't a particularly good student, mainly because she did not like the grind of the intellectual courses and preferred the many opportunities college presented socially. She talked her father into sending her back home to Los Angeles to visit relatives and friends. She heard that Paramount was shooting a film called *Monte Carlo* and she landed a part as an extra. This was accomplished by simply getting into a line of extras checking in for the film.

She persuaded Central Casting to register her but couldn't get another part and she started commuting to Pasadena evenings. She couldn't get on the stage of the Community Playhouse but did get into amateur plays at the workshop. She did land a part in *Follow Through* for Paramount in 1930, and her work convinced the studio officials that she had what it takes and they signed her to a long-term contract and signed her to play a French girl opposite Maurice Chevalier in *The* *Playboy of Paris.*

Later the depression disclosed that through a corporate mix-up none of the Paramount players' contracts were legally binding. All the stars were asked to resign. Those who were dissatisfied with their roles had an out. She gambled on leaving Paramount and security—against the advice of her agent. She managed to sign with RKO at a big boost in salary.

Films in which the 5′ 3″ beauty appeared were *Along Came Youth, An American Tragedy, Rich Man's Folly, Love is a Racket, The Reckless Age, If I Had a Million, Little Women, Of Human Bondage, Becky Sharp, Souls at Sea, Wells Fargo, So Ends Our Night, Wheel of Fortune, A Man Betrayed, Mr. Scoutmaser,* and *Gypsy Colt.*

In 1933 she played opposite Joel McCrea in *One Man's Journey* and wound up eloping with him. Upon the advice of Will Rogers, a close friend of Joel's, they purchased a 1400 acre cattle ranch in San Fernando Valley and they moved in on Christmas Eve of 1934. Their marriage produced three sons. One of them, Jody, is active in motion pictures.

Brian Donlevy (1903–1972)

Brian Waldo Donlevy was born February 9, 1903, in Portadown, County Armagh, Ireland. His parents brought him to the United States when he was 10 months of age. He attended St. John's Military Academy in Delafield, Wisconsin. At 13, big for his age, he enlisted in the Army and became a bugler with the Wisconsin troops chasing Pancho Villa in Mexico. At 14, he fibbed his way into the Lafayette Escadrille. He was a sergeant-pilot during World War I with the French Aviation Force and at 17 was a veteran with two war wounds.

After the war he was able to go through four years of studies in two, and won an appointment to the U.S. Naval Academy at Annapolis, but he left after only a year to try the stage. He had become interested in acting through the Academy theatrics. He went to New York City and success came slowly. He supplemented his income by posing for collar and cigarette ads, among other things.

He was helped by actor Louis Wolheim to a small role as Corporal Gowdy in *What Price Glory* in 1924. Continuing his modeling, he also appeared on Broadway in such shows as *Three For One, The Milky Way, Life Begins at 8:40, The Boy Friend,* and *Hit the Deck.* He landed a small part in his first film in 1929 for Pathe called *Mother's Boy.* His second film was *Gentlemen of the Press,* the same year, for Paramount. He did not appear on the screen again until 1935.

In 1935 he made his third film, *Barbary Coast,* for United Artists. In the film he portrayed the "killer," which was the start of many villainous portrayals that distinguished some of Hollywood's finest motion pictures. These included his role as Gil Warren in *In Old Chicago* in 1938, Barshee in *Jesse James,* Sid Campeau in *Union Pacific,* Kent in *Destry Rides Again* in 1939. Another film in 1939, *Beau Geste,* in which he played the sadistic Sergeant MarKoff earned for him a nomination for Best Supporting Actor.

He also played heroes in many "B" films in the 1930s, and after his success in Paramount's *The Great McGinty* in 1940 he graduated to better roles and was a likable hero all through the 40s.

Some of his other films include *36 Hours to Kill, This Is My Affair, I Wanted Wings, Hold Back the Dawn, Billy the Kid, Wake Island, The Glass Key, Stand By For Action, The Miracle of Morgan's Creek, Two Years Before the Mast, Heaven Only Knows,* and *Command Decision.*

In 1952 he played Steve Mitchell, the soldier of fortune in "Dangerous Assgnment" on television. He continued his motion picture career throughout the fifties and sixties. He died April 5, 1972, of throat cancer at the Motion Picture Country Hospital in Woodland Hills, California.

Brian Donlevy with Walter Pidgeon in Command
Decision *(MGM, 1948).*

Paul Douglas with Linda Darnell in A Letter to Three Wives *(20th Century-Fox, 1949).*

Paul Douglas (1907–1959)

Paul Douglas was born in Philadelphia April 11, 1907. He was orphaned when quite young and worked at odd jobs to support himself. Following graduation from West Philadelphia High School, he attended Yale University for two years where he was active in little-theater dramatics. After leaving Yale he played professional football with the Frankford, Pennsylvania, Yellow Jackets. He then turned to radio in 1930 where he became a sports announcer. He was a contemporary of sports announcer Bill Stern. Douglas broadcast more than a thousand baseball games for NBC and CBS.

From sportscasting he turned to commercial broadcasts and was the announcer for "The Jack Benny Program," "Easy Aces," "Burns and Allen," "The Fred Waring Show," "The Chesterfield Supper Club," "Buck Rogers in the 25th Century," "Jack Armstrong, the All-American Boy," "The True Story Hour with Mary and Bob" as well as other programs.

He was on stage in 1935 in *Double Dummy* and in 1946 he made his Broadway stage debut in *Born Yesterday* with Judy Holliday. He starred in 1024 performances before coming to Hollywood to make his first film, undertaking a starring role in 20th Century-Fox *A Letter to Three Wives,* which immediately established him on the screen. Other films include *It Happens Every Spring, Panic In the Streets, Fourteen Hours, Guy Who Came Back, Angels In the Outfield, When In Rome, Clash By Night, We're Not Married, Never Wave At a Wac, Forever Female, Executive Suite,* and *Joe MacBeth.* In his later years on the screen he made pictures in Austria, England, and Italy.

He was married to actress Virginia Field and they were divorced in 1947. In 1950 he married actress Jan Sterling. He completed starring in two half-hour TV shows, "The Incorrigibles" and "Casey at the Bat" on Rod Serling's "Twilight Zone" and was slated to co-star in Billy Wilder's *The Apartment* when he died at his home of a heart attack while getting out of bed on September 11, 1959.

James Dunn (1905–1967)

James Dunn was born in New York City, November 2, 1905. He appeared on Broadway in *Sweet Adeline* and other plays before coming to Hollywood in 1931.

He was signed by 20th Century-Fox and made several films with Sally Eilers such as *Don't Get Personal, Bad Girl, Over the Hill,* and *Dance Team*. His popularity was also helped by his appearances with Shirley Temple. In her first big film he tap danced with her; this was *Stand Up and Cheer* in 1934. He also appeared with her in *Bright Eyes* and *Baby Take a Bow*. Other films included *Handle With Care, Change of Heart, The Daring Young Man, Welcome Home,* and *Pride of the Navy*.

His popularity waned as a leading man in the early 1940s. In addition, he had earned the reputation as an irresponsible performer partly due to his drinking. This made him almost an untouch-able by all of the studios. In the mid 40s 20th Century-Fox was about to shoot the film version of Betty Smith's best-selling novel *A Tree Grows In Brooklyn*. Darryl Zanuck took a chance on him and brought him back into the fold at 20th Century-Fox to play Peggy Ann Garner's hard-drinking but kind-hearted father for the film version. His portrayal brought momentary fame as he won the Oscar for the Best Supporting Actor. He was allowed another part in another Fox film, but his role was small and he dropped out of sight of the film industry.

He returned to the stage, but was unsuccessful. From 1954 to 1956 he returned to Hollywood to co-star with Michael O'Shea and William Bishop on television in "It's A Great Life." After the show went off the air he had guest shots on TV and made an occasional film but he was no longer in demand. He died September 1, 1967.

James Dunn with Florence Rice in **The Ghost and the Guest** *(PRC, 1943).*

Dan Duryea (1907–1968)

Dan Duryea was an actor famed for his roles as an appealing heel. Duryea was typed throughout his career as a villain, and movie fans resisted his efforts to alter the image. Off the screen, however, he was known as a dedicated father and husband who loved children, flowers, and sailing craft. Duryea was a graduate of Cornell University where he succeeded Franchot Tone as president of the Dramatic Society. He first entered the advertising business but after a serious illness he turned to acting as a less strenuous occupation. His first stage role was as one of the G-men in the Broadway production of *Dead End*. After two years in that part, he was given a lead. Later he appeared as the half-witted Leo Hubbard in Lillian Hellman's *The Little Foxes*.

He made his first screen appearance in the film version in 1941 for Samuel Goldwyn. Instantly established as a heel, most of his future screen roles were of this genre, although occasionally he played comedy roles. In all, Duryea was in about 60 films, the last being *The Bamboo Saucer*. Among his film credits were *Pride of the Yankees*, *Sahara*, *Ministry of Fear*, *The Great Flamarion*, *The Valley of Decision*, *Another Part of the Forest*, *Winchester '73*, *Battle Hymn*, *The Flight of the Phoenix*, and *Five Golden Dragons*.

His entry into television opened up a new career for him. For several seasons his "China Smith" was one of the most popular series. He won an Emmy nomination in 1957 for his portrayal of the simple backwoodsman in General Electric's "The Road That Led Afar." He had wide exposure on television and starred in more than 75 television shows. Duryea also played the part of Eddie Jacks in the *Peyton Place* series.

A perfectionist in his profession, Duryea frequently worked all night perfecting his lines for the next day's shooting. Like so many screen heavies, he was the mildest of men, enjoying a full home life with his wife of 36 years, Helen, who preceded him in death in 1967. His hobby was building boats and racing on Lake Arrowhead, where he maintained a sumptuous mountain house. He lived quietly in a Hollywood hilltop house and rarely attended parties or visited nightclubs.

Dan Duryea with Dorothy Lamour in Manhandled (Paramount, 1949).

Ann Dvorak (1912–   )

Ann Dvorak was born Ann McKim in New York City August 12, 1912. Her mother was Ann Lehr, a professional actress, and her father, Sam McKim, was a director at Biograph.

Her early years were spent in a convent called St. Catherine's in New York. Her family later moved to California and Ann reportedly appeared in a few silents under her real name. After she graduated from the Page School in Los Angeles, she had a brief fling as a reporter. She was hired by MGM as a chorus dancer and although she knew nothing about dancing she became a dance instructress in only four months.

She appeared in several films for MGM, mostly as a chorus girl, from 1929 through 1931. Howard Hughes wanted a lead for *Scarface* for United Artists and Ann was recommended and her performance got her a contract from Warner Bros. Some of her Warner Bros. films included *Three on a Match, The Way to Lose, Massacre, Heat Lightning, Side Streets, Housewife, Gentlemen are Born, Murder in the Clouds, Dr. Socrates,* and *The G-Men.*

Her large, oval, captivating eyes were her best feature and overshadowed her nose, which by today's standard was much too large. She was at home in almost any type of role, but her early career was stymied at times by her temperament that led to many suspensions at Warner Bros. At this time she also eloped with actor Leslie Fenton, and during her bouts with Warners they would take off for Europe or wherever they felt like going. She felt that her parts weren't right or the film was poor and she and Warner Bros. finally parted company. Many of her parts even stand up well today.

She started appearing in films for other studios and these included *We Who Are About to Die, Racing Lady, She's No Lady, Gangs of New York, Blind Alley, Stronger than Desire, Cafe Hostess,* and *Girls of the Road.*

When World War II came along Fenton went to England and joined the British Navy, and she engrossed herself in helping the war effort on the home front and even made a few films.

After the war she appeared in *Flame of the Barbary Coast, Abilene Town, The Long Night, The Walls of Jericho, Our Very Own, A Life of Her Very Own, The Return of Jesse James, Mrs. O'Malley and Mr. Malone,* and her last *I Was An American Spy* in 1951.

She divorced Fenton in 1944 and married dancer Igor de Navrotsky in 1947. This marriage also ended in divorce and husband no. 3 became architect Nicholas Wade and they spend a great deal of time traveling.

Ann Dvorak with Preston Foster and John Beal in
We Who Are About to Die *(RKO, 1936).*

Stu Erwin with Marvin Stephens and Jane Withers in
Checkers *(20th Century-Fox, 1937).*

Stu Erwin (1903–1967)

Stuart Erwin was born on a ranch in Squaw Valley, California, and went to Los Angeles in the 1920s after becoming interested in dramatics while attending the University of California at Berkeley. His first professional stage appearance was in *The Open Gates* at the Morosco in Los Angeles. After a year in the part, he toured in *White Collars* and, thanks to Edward Everett Horton, was signed for several plays including *Beggar on Horseback*. While playing in *Women Go On Forever* at the Music Box in Hollywood, he signed for his first film role: the 1928 *Mother Knows Best.*

Put under contract by Fox Films, he made many films including *The Cockeyed World, Speakeasy, This Thing Called Love, Dude Ranch, Playboy of Paris, The Crime of the Century, The Big Broadcast, Make Me A Star, Palooka, Viva Villa,* *Exclusive Story,* and *Ceiling Zero.* He starred in *Pigskin Parade,* which also introduced Judy Garland, and played Howie Newsome in the 1940 film version of *Our Town.* Other roles included *When the Daltons Rode, The Bride Came C.O.D., Drums of the Congo, He Hired the Boss, Strike It Rich,* and *Heaven Only Knows.*

Erwin returned to the stage in 1942 and played opposite Lillian Gish in *Mr. Sycamore.* In the early 1950s he and his wife, actress June Collyer, appeared on television in "The Trouble With Father," which later became "The Stu Erwin Show." Erwin was semiretired in the 1960s but did make several television appearances. He died suddenly of a heart attack in his Beverly Hills home on December 21, 1967.

49

Frances Farmer (1910–1970)

Frances Farmer had a Hollywood career mixed with success and personal tragedy—her private and professional life read like a weekday soap opera. Miss Farmer graduated from West Seattle High School in 1931 and was active in drama at the University of Washington. Her first break came in 1935 as an indirect result of a trip to Moscow, a prize she won for selling subscriptions to a Seattle leftist newspaper. On board ship she was introduced to producer Sherpart Traube. Through him, she signed a seven-year contract with Paramount, which got her the lead in the film version of Edna Ferber's *Come and Get It*. This was followed by being cast on Broadway in Clifford Odet's *Golden Boy*. Her other films included *Ebb Tide, The Toast of New York, Ride a Crooked Mile, South of Pago Pago, World Premiere, Among the Living, Son of Fury,* and *The Party Crashers* in 1958.

After her film career was well under way, she became difficult to work with and she began to drink heavily. She spent a number of years after 1942 in mental hospitals. In 1950, she returned to her hometown of Seattle under an assumed name and worked as a maid in the Olympic Hotel. Later she worked as a room clerk at the Sheraton-Palace in San Francisco. In 1957 she made a modified comeback with a few stage and television roles. In 1958 she moved to Indianapolis where she hosted a television film program for several years.

She also served as an actress-in-residence at Purdue University. In 1964, she was named Indiana Businesswoman of the Year. On August 1, 1970, she died of cancer of the esophagus in Indianapolis. In 1972 her extraordinary autobiography, *Will There Really Be a Morning?*, was

Frances Farmer in **Badlands of Dakota** *(Universal, 1941).*

published. Miss Farmer had stipulated that all proceeds from this book were to go into a special fund set up to help decorate and brighten state asylums throughout the United States.

Glenda Farrell with John Butler in Torchy Runs For Mayor *(Warner Bros., 1939).*

Glenda Farrell (1904–1971)

Glenda Farrell appeared in more than a hundred movies usually cast as the dizzy, fun-loving, gum-chewing, wisecracking blonde. She was born on June 30, 1904, in Enid, Oklahoma, and studied at Mount Carmel Academy in Wichita, Kansas. Her earliest ambition was to go on the stage, and after leaving school she joined a stock company. She appeared with the Virginia Brissac Stock Company in San Diego from 1918 until 1920. Later she was a member of the Morosco Stock Company in Los Angeles. She worked her way to Broadway and made her first appearance as Marion Hardy in *Skidding* in 1928, which later became Hollywood's Andy Hardy series. She had a successful Broadway career. In 1930 her role as a gangster's moll, Marie Pouliski, in the hit, *On the Spot,* propelled her into that of Olga in the movie *Little Caesar* with Edward G. Robinson.

Miss Farrell teamed with Joan Blondell in the Golddiggers film series and also made a hit in the Torchy Blane series. Some of her other movie roles included *I Am a Fugitive from a Chain Gang, Hi, Nellie, Talk of the Town, Johnny Eager, Lulu Belle, Susan Slept Here, Middle of the Night,* and *The Disorderly Orderly.* Her television career included winning an Emmy as Best Supporting Actress in 1963 for a role on an episode of the "Ben Casey" show. She was also seen on "Wagon Train," "Bonanza," "The Fugitive," "The Defenders," and "Dr. Kildare," among others. She also commuted regularly to Broadway to appear in such plays as *Separate Rooms, The Overtons,* and *Home Is the Hero.*

Her last appearance on Broadway was in the hit play, *Forty Carats,* in 1968. She became ill during the run of the show, and never fully recovered. She died on May 1, 1971, at her home in New York.

51

Dick Foran (1910–   )

Dick Foran was born John Nicholas Foran on June 18, 1910, in Flemington, New Jersey. His father, Colonel Arthur F. Foran, was chairman of the New Jersey Highway Commission, former comptroller of the Port of New York, a banker, iron founder, and director of steamship and railway companies. He later became the Republican senator from New Jersey. As a youth young Nicholas worked in the foundry and also on his father's farm in Flemington. He was educated at the Hun School, and then attended Princeton University where he was a tackle on the Princeton Eleven.

After graduation from Princeton he was interested in becoming a geologist but also was fond of singing and he studied music at the Leibling studio in New York and he got his chance to sing over the radio. He was heard for a time as the vocalist on the "Burns and Allen Show." He formed his own orchestra but disbanded due to difficulty in securing bookings.

He went to Hollywood and Lew Brown, an old family friend, was casting for *Stand Up and Cheer* for Fox; he gave him a test and a part in the film. The year was 1934 and at the time he used the name Nick Foran as he did in his second film *Gentlemen Are Born* for First National. Still using the name Nick Foran the following year he appeared in several Fox films: *One More Spring, Lottery Lover, It's a Small World,* and *Ladies Love Danger.* He changed his name to Dick Foran in *Shipmates Forever* for First National the same year. He was also placed under contract to Warner Bros.

In 1935, Gene Autry became a sensation as a singing cowboy for Republic and Warners wanted someone to compete in this field. They chose Foran on the basis of his singing and athletic abilities. The films were fairly well made and in 1935 he appeared in *Moonlight on the Prairie.* The following year his western features were *Song of the Saddle, Treachery Rides the Range,* and *Trailin' West.*

In 1937 his films were *Guns of the Pecos, Cherokee Strip, Land Beyond the Law,* and *Devil's Saddle Legion.* For his efforts he was voted among the Top 10 in western stars for 1936 and 1937. In 1940 he starred in the Universal serial *Winners of the West* and in 1941 also starred in another serial *Riders of Death Valley,* which was notable for its ambitious cast that included Buck Jones, Leo Carrillo, and Charles Bickford.

Since his starring western films he has starred or co-starred in many features playing a variety of roles, and later he switched to character parts. His films include *The Mummy's Hand, In the Navy, The Mummy's Tomb, Guest Wife, Fort Apache, Al Jennings of Oklahoma, Violent Road, Donovan's Reef, Taggart,* and *Brighty of the Grand Canyon.* He has made many TV appearances and is still active.

Dick Foran with Claudette Colbert in Guest Wife
(United Artists, 1945).

Preston Foster with Jeff Donnell and Coleen Gray in
Destination 60,000 (Allied Artists, 1957).

Preston Foster (1902–1970)

Preston Foster was born in Ocean City, New Jersey, on August 24, 1902. He was raised in Pitman and after high school he worked as a bus driver, shipping clerk, ad salesman, and a professional wrestler. He had a fine basso voice and he landed a stage role as a spear-carrying super with the Philadelphia Grand Opera. He was given more important parts in such stage plays as *Two Seconds* and *The Silent House.*

He landed a part in the film *Heads Up* for Paramount in 1930, but his real break came when Mervyn LeRoy saw his performance on Broadway in *Two Seconds* and signed him for the same part in the film. He was signed to a Warner Bros. contract and in 1932 he played the part of Killer Mears in Wide World's *The Last Mile.* For Warner Bros. he appeared in *I Am a Fugitive From a Chain Gang, The All-American, Elmer the Great,* and *Heat Lightning.* He then signed with RKO in 1935 and appeared in *People's Enemy, The Informer, The Arizonian, Last Days of Pompeii, Annie Oakley,* and *Outcasts of Poker Flat.* He later free-lanced and his many films included *Up the River, Geronimo, North West Mounted Police, My Friend Flicka, Guadalcanal Diary, Roger Touhy, Gangster, The Harvey Girls, I Shot Jesse James,* and *Montana Territory.* During his career he was equally at home as the hero or the villain.

The very talented Foster also was a composer and wrote *To Shillelagh O'Sullivan* with Perry Bolkin, and this was recorded by Bing Crosby. He also wrote the official song of the San Diego Baseball team, *Let's Go Padres.* From 1949 to 1957 he taught his actress wife, Sheila D'Arcy, how to sing, taught himself to play the guitar, and they toured night clubs with their own brand of folk music and comedy.

In 1953 he added television to his list of laurels as he starred as Captain Herrick in "Waterfront" and he also starred as the commanding officer in "The Gunslinger" telepix.

In his later years he was active in real estate ventures, yacht sales, and he devoted much time to Coast Guard Auxiliary activities. He died on July 14, 1970, of a heart attack in La Jolla, California.

Kay Francis (1903–1968)

Kay Francis became famous for her roles as "the other woman" as well as her more popular roles depicting frustrated mother love. She was one of Hollywood's leading glamour girls in the 1930s and 1940s, partial to long, slinky, low-cut gowns by night and lavishly-furred suits by day. She was considered one of Hollywood's best-dressed women and the epitome of glamour and sexiness in her era. She was born in Oklahoma City, Oklahoma, on January 13, 1903, and was the daughter of an actress, Katherine Clinton. Miss Francis took her stage name from her first husband, Dwight Francis.

Educated in convents, the tall, beautiful, gray-eyed brunette originally trained for a business career, but after a tour of Europe returned, determined to become an actress. She got her first role on Broadway as the player queen in the successful modern-dress version of *Hamlet* in 1925. Despite a speech defect (lallation) she became a successful actress and in 1930 she went to Hollywood to appear in *Gentlemen of the Press,* and remained to play in many films opposite many of Hollywood's most famous leading men including William Powell, Ronald Colman, Herbert Marshall, Cary Grant, Dick Powell, Don Ameche, and Leslie Howard.

Her other film credits included *Dangerous Curves, Paramount on Parade, Scandal Sheet, Man Wanted, I Loved a Woman, I Found Stella Parish, The White Angel, King of the Underworld, It's a Date, Little Men, Charley's Aunt, Four Jills in a Jeep, Allotment Wives,* and her last film *Wife Wanted*. She was a popular success and her financial rewards were substantial. In 1937 she received $227,500 in salary as Warner Brothers' highest paid contract player while an industrial executive like the chairman of the Firestone Tire and Rubber Company earned $85,000.

In 1945, she left Hollywood and toured in *Windy Hill* and then returned to Broadway in 1946 to succeed Ruth Hussey in *State of the Union*. She later played in several summer stock playhouses in the East. She never appeared on television. Inactive since 1952, her last years were spent in New York, and she summered near Falmouth, Cape Cod. On August 26, 1968, she died of cancer at her New York apartment. She left instructions that there be no funeral service, that her body be cremated and her ashes scattered to the winds. Most of her $1,000,000 estate was willed to Seeing Eye, Inc.

Kay Francis and William Gargan in Women In the Wind *(Warner Bros., 1939).*

Van Heflin (1910–1971)

Van Heflin gained fame as a character actor mostly in supporting roles. Tall and sandy-haired, he escaped being stereotyped as any one kind of character. He once said, "I've never played the same part twice, and no one has ever said 'This is a Heflin character' like they've said about Cary Grant and Clark Gable . . . I'm a character actor, always have been."

Born Emmet Evan Heflin, son of a dentist in Walters, Oklahoma, he was brought to Long Beach, California, by his parents when he was seven. In the seashore town, he became fascinated by the sea and, soon after high school graduation, hopped a freighter for New York. There, he met the director of Channing Pollock's *Mr. Money-penny* and in October, 1928, enjoyed his first Broadway credit playing Junior Jones in the play. He received a degree in dramatics from the University of Oklahoma in 1931 and a master's degree at the Yale School of Drama. He was an understudy in the Broadway musical *Sailor, Beware*. Three years later, with his rugged but boyish countenance and demonstrated stage talent, he starred with Katherine Hepburn and Joseph Cotten for a two-year run in *The Philadelphia Story*. This role won him in 1940 a contract from MGM.

He made his film debut in 1936 co-starring with Katherine Hepburn in *A Woman Rebels*. Heflin was quickly established in the film industry's thinking as a solid supporting character actor rather than a romantic lead. He received an Academy Award in 1942 for his role as a drunken scholar gone to seed in a gangster picture, *Johnny Eager*. He was quickly promoted to lead roles. In 1942 he married film actress Francis Neal, and went off to war serving as a combat photographer with the Ninth Air Force in Europe.

After the war, he returned to films and asked MGM in 1950 to release him from his contract. The studio did reduce his commitment to twelve weeks a year, and Heflin continued his career as one of the few actors able to maintain careers in more than one medium at once. He was a success on Broadway while still making movies and appearing in television dramas. Some of his notable screen appearances included *Shane, Battle Cry, A*

Van Heflin in Shane **(Paramount, 1953).**

Woman's World, They Came to Cordura, Green Dolphin Street, Madame Bovary, Black Widow, 3:10 to Yuma, Gunman's Walk, The Greatest Story Ever Told, and *Airport.* In the latter, he portrayed a disturbed passenger intent on blowing up an airliner.

His stardom never brought the adulation accorded actors who specialized as romantic leading men, but he was respected by other actors and seldom appeared in an unsuccessful film, either artistically or commercially. On June 6, 1971, he suffered a heart attack while swimming. He died on July 23 and left instructions that no public or private funeral be held, and that his remains be cremated and scattered over the Pacific Ocean, where he loved to sail and fish.

Paul Henreid (1908–   )

Paul Henreid was born Paul Hernried Ritter von Wasel-Waldingau January 10, 1908, in Trieste, Austria. He spent most of his childhood in Vienna where he later attended the exclusive Maria Theresianische Academie. Following his graduation he enrolled at the Academie of Graphic Arts, preparing to enter the publishing field. After graduation he joined the firm of Strobl, Vienna's leading book printers and publishers. Later he enrolled in night classes at the Konservatorium of Dramatic Arts and completed the two year course in one year. He attracted the attention of Max Reinhardt who offered him a year's contract at his Vienna Theatre. At the end of the second year Paul had become one of Vienna's most popular young actors.

His career brought him to London in 1935 where he lived for five years before coming to America. Here he appeared in plays as well as motion pictures.

Gilbert Miller, the American theatrical producer, saw Paul in *The Jersey Lily* in London and invited him to come to New York to repeat his London performance. He arrived in New York on August 12, 1940. The play was never produced. In 1941 he did portray Dr. Walter in *Flight To The West* and this role won for him the best performance on the Broadway Stage. He was also voted Best Actor in a Foreign Film by New York Critics that same year for *Night Train*.

He made his Hollywood screen debut in 1941 with Michele Morgan in *Joan of Paris* for RKO. He became a big box-office attraction, a romantic star with a brand of continental charm and courtly suavity that drove the ladies into the theaters. He gained a world-wide reputation as one of the cinema's top heart-throbbers. He started a national vogue by lighting two cigarettes simultaneously for Bette Davis in *Now, Voyager*. It became a trademark for Henreid, his debonair gesture.

He was under contract to Warner Brothers for six years. Some of the films that he starred in include *Casablanca, In Our Time, The Conspirators, Between Two Worlds, Of Human Bondage, Devotion, Song of Love, Hollow Triumph, Rope of Sand, Stolen Face, Never So Few,* and *The Madwoman of Chaillot.*

He later became one of the successful directors in Hollywood and has also produced many motion pictures. He returned to Broadway in 1955 to star in *Festival* and has also appeared many times on television. He has directed many television films following an offer from Alfred Hitchcock in 1957. He helmed more than 60 films for the Hitchcock series. He has also directed such television films as "Maverick," "Cheyenne," "The Big Valley," "Bonanza," "Bracken's World," and many others.

He definitely prefers the transition and says, "Directing is actually the wish of my life. And now, in this particular stage of my life, I find more creativity in the work of a director than of an actor. I feel more fulfilled as a picture maker than as an actor."

He has been happily married since 1936 and resides in Brentwood Park, Los Angeles.

Paul Henreid in Hollow Triumph *(Eagle-Lion, 1948).*

Irene Hervey with Lloyd Nolan and Robert Armstrong
in **Mr. Dynamite** *(Universal, 1941).*

Irene Hervey (1910–   )

Irene Hervey was born Irene Herwick on July 11, 1910 in Los Angeles, California. Her father, John L. Herwick, was a photographer. She grew up in Santa Monica, California and graduated from Venice High School. After graduation she enrolled in Egan's Dramatic School and appeared in many amateur shows.

She signed a four-year contract at MGM but could not obtain even a minute role at this studio. She made up her mind to leave and seek work elsewhere when she was given a substantial role in *Stranger's Return* as Franchot Tone's wife. This was in 1933. Her reviews were very good and this enabled her to obtain a variety of roles.

She made several films for MGM, did some free-lancing and then signed a Universal contract. Her nearly 60 film appearances include *His Night Out, Charlie Chan in Shanghai, Say it in French,* *East Side of Heaven, Destry Rides Again, The Boys from Syracuse, Unseen Enemy, Bombay Clipper, Frisco Lil, Manhandled, A Cry in the Night, Cactus Flower,* and *Play Misty for Me.* From 1933 through 1943 she made 45 of her films, but in 1943 she was in an automobile accident and suffered a broken kneecap forcing her to leave films for a while. Her film career resumed in 1948, but parts were not so plentiful.

After an unsuccessful earlier marriage in which a daughter was born she married Allan Jones in 1936. Their son, Jack Jones, who is a popular singer was born a couple of years later. In 1957 her marriage to Allan Jones terminated. Although her movie roles dwindled her career was zooming in television, where she appeared in several soap operas and many other shows.

John Hodiak (1914–1955)

John Hodiak was born April 16, 1914, in Pittsburgh, Pennsylvania. When he was very young the family moved to Hamtramck, Michigan. His entertainment career began at the age of 11 while a student in grammar schools where he acted in several Ukrainian plays staged by his local parish. While in high school his favorite sport was baseball and he was a good enough third baseman that he was offered a contract to play professionally for the St. Louis Cardinals. After much deliberation he turned down the offer to pursue an acting career.

He went to work for Chevrolet in Detroit in the stock room after graduation from high school. In the evenings he played small roles for a local Detroit radio station. Later he went to Chicago and tried out for the role of Li'l Abner. He got the part and his radio career began. From 1940 through 1942 he appeared on many radio programs including such daytime soap operas as "Arnold Grimm's Daughter," "Bachelor's Children," "Girl Alone," "Lone Journey," and "The Romance of Helen Trent." He also played the lead of Steve Benton in "Wings of Destiny" and had a role in "The Lone Ranger" in addition to many others.

Radio attracted the attention of Hollywood, and Hodiak was given a screen test and signed by MGM. His first role was in *A Stranger in Town* in 1943. This was followed by small roles in *I Dood It, Swing Shift Maisie,* and *Song of Russia.* His first loanout role was opposite Tallulah Bankhead in *Lifeboat* at 20th Century-Fox. His other films included *Sunday Dinner for a Soldier, A Bell for Adano, The Harvey Girls, Homecoming, Command Decision, Battleground,* and *Across the Wide Missouri.* His contract with MGM came to an end in 1952 and he became a free-lancer and made several more films including his last *On the Threshold of Space.* All in all he appeared in 34 films.

In 1946 he married actress Anne Baxter and in 1953 they were divorced. In 1954 he appeared on the New York stage in Paul Gregory's *The Caine Mutiny Court Martial* in which he received excellent reviews.

On October 19, 1955, while shaving, he died of a heart attack at the age of 41.

John Hodiak with Robert Stack in Conquest of Cochise (Columbia, 1953).

Judy Holliday with Jack Carson and Jack Lemmon in Phffft *(Columbia, 1954).*

Judy Holliday (1922–1965)

Judy Holliday was born Judith Tuvim, June 21, 1922, in New York City. Her parents were divorced when she was a child. Her mother was a piano teacher. She graduated from Julia Richman High School where she was an exceptionally intelligent student with an IQ of 172. She was active in dramatics and other extra-curricular activities.

Her first attempt to get into show business was with the Orson Welles and John Houseman Players at the Mercury theatre, but she only managed to land a job as a telephone operator. She later joined Betty Comden, Adolph Green, Alvin Hammer, and John Frank in the formation of a vocal group called The Revuers, which graduated from Greenwich Village to nightclubs and their act lasted for five years.

Her first stage role was a supporting one in *Kiss Them For Me* in 1945 and she won the Clarence Derwent award for Best Supporting Actress of the Year. She got her big chance when illness forced Jean Arthur to withdraw from the starring role in *Born Yesterday* three days before its Philadelphia opening. The part was given to Holliday and she learned her role in just 72 hours. Her role drew sensational audience reaction and spectacular critical notices when the show reached Broadway. It was a dream come true and she played the role for three years and 1200 performances.

In spite of her stage success, when Columbia decided to make a film from the popular Garson Kanin comedy she was not in the running as a contender for the dumb-but-smart Billie Dawn. She finally got the part and starred opposite Broderick Crawford. Her performance in the film won for her the coveted Oscar as the top actress and her competition for this prize consisted of Bette Davis, Anne Baxter, Eleanor Parker, and Gloria Swanson.

Her film career actually began in 1942 without much fanfare as she appeared in *Something for the Boys*. Her other films were *Winged Victory, Greenwich Village, Adam's Rib, The Marrying Kind, It Should Happen to You, Phffft!, Solid Gold Cadillac, Full of Life,* and *Bells Are Ringing.*

She was also the 1956-1957 winner of the Best Femme Performance in a Broadway musical by the New York Drama Critics for her portrayal in *Bells Are Ringing.*

She was married in 1948 to David Oppenheim, a clarinetist and head of the classical division of Columbia Records. They had a son but were divorced in 1957. The very popular actress was plagued by cancer for several years and had undergone surgery. She entered Mt. Sinai Hospital in New York on May 26, 1965 and died of throat cancer on June 7, 1965.

Rochelle Hudson with Edward Norris in Show Them
No Mercy *(20th Century-Fox, 1935).*

Rochelle Hudson (1914–1972)

Rochelle Hudson was born March 6, 1914, in Oklahoma City, Oklahoma. When she was three years old she began to take dancing lessons. She moved to Hollywood with her parents when she was 13, where she came under the tutelage of Ernest Belcher. He turned her over to the voice coach of 20th Century-Fox. Although the studio did feel she had the potential to become a star she received no roles and they dropped her option.

Her first screen role was a small one in *Laugh and Get Rich* with Edna Mae Oliver in 1931. She then appeared in *Fanny Foley Herself* and *Are These Our Children* in the same year, and her screen career was launched. Her greatest popularity was in 1930s and very early 40s and she appeared in over 75 films, which included *Harold Teen, Judge Priest, Imitation of Life, The Mighty Barnum, Les Miserables, She Done Him Wrong, Curly Top, Show Them No Mercy, Way Down East, Island of Doomed Men, Rebel Without a Cause,* and *Strait-Jacket.*

The petite 5′ 4″ Hudson was never really happy in Hollywood and felt she never received the type of roles that were suited for her. After 1942, roles were scarce. She appeared with Bert Lahr on Broadway in 1950 and she made 39 episodes for television for "That's My Boy" with Eddie Mayehoff from 1954 to 1955.

In 1969 she opened her own real estate brokerage firm. She was married three times, all ending in divorce. The first was to Disney Story Editor Hal Thompson; that ended in divorce in 1947. Her second was to sportswriter Dick Hyland and was divorced in 1950. The third was to hotel executive Robert Mindell, and the marriage terminated January 8, 1972. Nine days later she was found dead at her Palm Desert, California, home by a real estate business associate.

Rita Johnson (1912–1965)

Rita Johnson specialized in "the other woman" roles. Her career began in New York where she did some plays and was active in radio in the early 1930s including *Joyce Jordan, Girl Intern*. In 1937 she appeared in George M. Cohan's *Fulton of Fall Oaks* for which she attracted the attention of MGM, where she received a contract. Her first movie was *London By Night*. During her career, her best performances were probably as Ray Milland's fiancé in *The Major and the Minor*, as Robert Young's wife in *They Won't Believe Me*, and as the murder victim in *The Big Clock*. Her film career was virtually ended in 1948 by an accident in her Los Angeles home. She was injured when a hairdryer collapsed on her head, causing a blood clot that was removed only after delicate brain surgery. Her left side was temporarily paralyzed, and for a time she was unable to walk. After the accident, she appeared only infrequently in films, her last appearance being in *All Mine To Give* in 1957. Her other film credits included *Man-Proof, Rich Man-Poor Girl, Honolulu, Broadway Serenade, Nick Carter, Master Detective, Edison, The Man, Here Comes Mr. Jordan, My Friend Flicka, The Affairs of Susan, Sleep, My Love, Family Honeymoon*, and *Unchained*. On October 31, 1965, she died at County General Hospital in Hollywood.

Rita Johnson with George Murphy in London By Night *(MGM, 1937).*

Nancy Kelly (1921–   )

Nancy Kelly was born in Lowell, Massachusetts, on March 25, 1921. Her education included the Immaculate Conception Academy in New York, St. Lawrence Academy in Long Island, and the Bentley School for Girls. Her mother, the former Nan Walsh, was an actress who longed to be on the professional stage. Her father was Jack Kelly, who was in the theater brokerage business.

She never attended dramatic school. Her mother did not tell Nancy bedtime stories when she was young; they would act them out. In this manner she was taught all the emotions necessary to become an actress. When her mother thought she was at the point that she could register any emotion she talked to the casting director at a Long Island studio. Gloria Swanson was looking for a child to play in *The Untamed Lady* for Paramount. She was interviewed and got the part. This was in 1926 and at the age of four her career was launched. She made many films as a juvenile including *Say It Again* for Paramount with Richard Dix in 1926 and *Mismates* with Warner Baxter the same year, where they cemented a lasting friendship.

By the time that she was five years of age she was known as "America's Most Photographed Child" and it was difficult to pick up a magazine without seeing her face in advertisements. She appeared in a number of Red Seal comedies in which she was a feminine Tom Mix Junior, riding horses and doing daredevil stunts. By the time

that she was eight years old she had appeared in 52 films. Her last film as a youngster was *The Girl on the Barge* in 1929. As she got older she became chubby and went on the radio. She was the first ingenue to appear on the *March of Time* program. She was Dorothy on "The Wizard of Oz" broadcasts for six months and played Nancy Miller on the "Myrt and Marge" broadcasts. She appeared on Broadway in *Give Me Yesterday*. She was Gertrude Lawrence's daughter in the Broadway stage play *Susan and God* in 1937. She left the play and came to Hollywood. Her screen test convinced every Hollywood producer that they needed her but she decided on 20th Century-Fox, as they had fewer young actresses. Her first film for the studio as a young adult was in *Submarine Patrol*. She was then given the plum role of Tyrone Power's wife in *Jesse James* when only 17 years of age.

Other films followed including *Stanley and Livingstone, Tail Spin, Frontier Marshal, He Married His Wife, One Night in the Tropics, Scotland Yard, To the Shores of Tripoli, Friendly Enemies, Tarzan's Desert Mystery, Show Business, Song of the Sarong, Betrayal from the East, Disaster,* and *The Bad Seed*. She was one child star who also made the grade as an adult.

Her brother, Jack, also appeared in Broadway plays and early films but achieved greater success on television in the popular "Maverick" series as Bart Maverick. He also appeared in films.

Nancy Kelly with Johnny Sheffield and Johnny Weiss-muller in **Tarzan's Desert Mystery** *(RKO, 1943).*

Paul Kelly (1899–1956)

Paul Kelly was born August 9, 1899, in Brooklyn, New York. He made his first professional appearance on the stage at the age of seven and was also an actor at the old Vitagraph Studios in Flatbush. He later played in such stage plays as *Penrod* and *Seventeen* in 1918, *Up the Ladder* and *Whispering Wives* in 1922, and *Chains* in 1923.

His own life took on the overtones of a Hollywood scenario in 1927. He had long been in love with an actress named Dorothy MacKaye since his childhood days. He administered a brutal and fatal beating to Miss MacKaye's first husband, Roy Raymond, an early-day musical comedy star. He was tried in Los Angeles on a murder charge, but convicted of manslaughter and sentenced to five years in San Quentin. He served two years of his sentence and was paroled, and Miss MacKaye served a 10-month sentence for conspiring to withhold information concerning her husband's death. After Kelly's parole he resumed his career and appeared on the stage in 1931 in *Bad Girl*. He married Dorothy MacKaye the same year.

In 1933 he appeared in his first film, *Broadway Through a Keyhole,* for United Artists. He starred in many films was featured in many others and in his later years turned to character parts. His films include *The President Vanishes, Public Hero No. 1, Here Comes Trouble, Join the Marines, Happened Out West, The Missing Guest, Queen of the Mob, Girls Under 21, Mystery Ship, Flying Tigers, The Story of Dr. Wassell, The Glass Alibi,* and his last *Bailout at 43,000.*

He also continued his stage career appearing in *Beggers Are Coming to Town* in 1945, *Command Decision* in 1947, and *The Country Girl* in 1950. In 1940, the woman he had gone to prison for was killed in an automobile accident near their Northridge ranch.

Paul Kelly with Sally Eilers in Nurse from Brooklyn *(Universal, 1938).*

On November 6, 1956 he returned home after casting his vote in the Eisenhower-Stevenson presidential election. He suffered a fatal heart attack which was his third in the last three years. His second wife, former actress Clare Owen, was with him when he was pronounced dead.

Patric Knowles with Paul Cavanagh in Flame of Calcutta *(Columbia, 1953).*

Patric Knowles (1911–   )

Patric Knowles was born Reginald Lawrence Knowles on November 11, 1911, in Leeds, England. He attended various schools in Oxford, England, then joined his father in his advertising and publishing business in Oxford. After several amateur appearances on the stage in Oxford, he decided to make a career of acting and left the advertising and publishing business to go to London where he joined Anew McMaster's Shakespearean Players, opening at the Theatre Royal in Margate, England, on February 3, 1931. The play was *Othello.*

The same company played the Abbey Theatre, Dublin, for twelve weeks, then toured Ireland for fourteen months. Plays presented were *Hamlet, Romeo and Juliet, MacBeth, As You Like It, She Stoops to Conquer, Mister Wu,* and *Importance of Being Earnest,* among others.

After touring the British Isles and Ireland, he returned to London to appear on the stage and he appeared in many noteworthy plays. In March of 1935, Irving Asher of Warner Brothers of England signed him to a term contract and after a dozen films sent him to Hollywood to play Errol Flynn's brother in *The Charge of the Light Bri-*

gade. He remained in the United States to make over seventy motion pictures.

He has been under term contract to Warner Bros., Republic, RKO, Universal, and Paramount at various times. Included among his films are *Robin Hood, Four's A Crowd, Heart of the North, Storm Over Bengal, A Bill of Divorcement, Five Came Back, Another Thin Man, How Green Was My Valley, Three Came Home, The Wolf Man, Ivy, Kitty, Of Human Bondage, Auntie Mame, The Way West,* and *Chisum.* He has also made many television appearances.

During World War II, he served as a flying instructor in the R.C.A.F. and later, in the same capacity with the U.S.A.A.F. He married the former Enid Percival of Purley, England, on October 3, 1935. They have two children, Michael and Antonia.

His interests are golf, sailing, flying, riding, long walks, and swimming. From 1952 until 1955 he served as honorary mayor of Tarzana, California, and was vice-president of the Woodland Hills Country Club in 1951. He also wrote and published a novel, *Even Steven,* in 1960.

Carole Landis (1919–1948)

Carole Landis was born Frances Lillian Mary Ridste on January 1, 1919, in Fairchild, Wisconsin. A beautiful girl with a curvaceous figure, she became a model and then became a singer with a band. She came to Hollywood after several stage plays in New York and her career was anything but sensational in her early years.

She had many bit roles in films including several westerns and did not get her first break until 1940 when she was given the lead in *One Million B.C.* Even though she had no dialogue she was on the screen long enough to convince Hollywood that she had what it takes to become a star and her career in films from that point on was meteoric. She had appeared virtually unnoticed in 17 previous films.

Following *One Million B.C.* she was in *Turnabout, Road Show, Topper Returns, Dance Hall, Moon Over Miami, I Wake Up Screaming, Cadet Girl, A Gentleman at Heart, It Happened in Flatbush, My Gal Sal, Orchestra Wives, Manila Calling, The Powers Girl, Wintertime, Secret Command,* and *Four Jills in a Jeep.*

When World War II came along she was one of the first to entertain the troops. Her health suffered as she contracted amoebic dysentery and malaria. Her experiences during the war enabled her to write *Four Jills in a Jeep* in which she co-starred in 1944 with Kay Francis, Martha Raye, and Mitzi Mayfair.

She was not as popular when she returned to Hollywood and her last few films were hardly worth noticing. She turned to the New York stage in 1945 and appeared in the play *A Lady Says Yes.*

Like many of the beautiful stars of the past she had many disappointments. Four marriages failed and she had an unsuccessful romance with actor Rex Harrison. Her career was definitely on the decline and she was only 29 years old. On July 5, 1948, she was found dead in her home in Hollywood by Rex Harrison, apparently a suicide caused by an overdose of sleeping pills.

Carole Landis with Joan Blondell and Dennis O'Keefe
in **Topper Returns** *(United Artists, 1941).*

*Priscilla Lane with George Humbert and May Robson
in* Daughters Courageous *(Warner Bros., 1939).*

Priscilla Lane (1917–   )

Priscilla Lane was born Priscilla Mullican on June 12, 1917, in Indianola, Iowa. Her father was a dentist and her mother was a reporter on the local paper with an ambition to become a big city reporter. Instead she became a small town housewife with five daughters: Leota, Martha, Lola, Rosemary, and the youngest, Priscilla.

All of the girls had talent and under the careful guidance of their mother they all got their chance for a certain amount of fame. The best conservatory of music in the state, Simpson College, was located in their community. Leota was the first in the family to achieve some success singing at Chautauqua and conventions throughout the state. While visiting Des Moines she met Gus Edwards, he listened to her sing and presented her with a contract. Lola was also signed by Edwards at the same time. Upon his advice the entire family changed their last name to Lane.

Martha married a local professor and sold verses to national magazines. Rosemary and Priscilla were still home and they ventured to Des Moines on weekends to study dancing. They went to New York for a family reunion and while singing in a New York publishing house they were heard by Fred Waring. He signed them and for four-and-a-half years they toured the U.S.A. with his band, with radio appearances in between.

Hollywood sent for Waring's Pennsylvanians to appear in Warner Bros.' *Varsity Show* in 1937. Both girls signed long-term contracts with the studio before filming was completed. Priscilla stayed with Warner Bros. for most of her film career, and her films include *Men Are Such Fools, Four Daughters, Brother Rat, Yes, My Darling Daughter, Daughters Courageous, Dust Be My Destiny, The Roaring Twenties, Four Wives, Brother Rat and a Baby, Four Mothers, Blues In the Night,* and *Arsenic and Old Lace.*

Her last screen appearance was in *Bodyguard* for RKO in 1948. She combined a certain beguiling innocence with a certain amount of mischief that made her very popular with audiences during her 11-year career.

She married Oren Hoagland in 1939 and was divorced in 1940. She married Joseph Howard in 1942.

Anita Louise (1917–1970)

Anita Louise in Glamour For Sale *(Columbia, 1940).*

baby was so beautiful that artists begged her parents to permit her to pose. As a child, Miss Louise first became famous as the "Post Toasties Girl." She was educated at the Professional Children's School. At the age of five, she appeared in her first movie *Sixth Commandment,* and appeared on the Broadway stage in *Peter Ibbetson* a year later. At thirteen, she played her first grown-up role in *Just Like Heaven.*

As a contract player for Warner Brothers and Columbia Pictures, she appeared in such movies as *The Floradora Girl, Madame du Barry, A Midsummer Night's Dream, The Story of Louis Pasteur, Anthony Adverse, The Green Light, Marie Antoinette, The Sisters, Casanova Brown, The Fighting Guardsman, The Bandit of Sherwood Forest,* and *Retreat, Hell!* Her first husband was producer Buddy Adler, who became production chief at 20th Century-Fox after their marriage in 1940. He died in 1960, and in 1962 she married businessman Henry Berger.

Her last widely known role was in the television series "My Friend Flicka" in the 1950s, but she later made guest appearances on the "Mannix" and "Mod Squad" television series. Although not acting in films in recent years, she was a favorite in Hollywood, known for her regal bearing and for elaborate parties in her plush home in Holmsby Hills.

On April 25, 1970, she died of a brain hemorrhage. Her funeral services were attended by many in Hollywood. Her pallbearers included actors Henry Fonda, Anthony Quinn, Ricardo Montalban, Jim Backus, and Robert Stack. Stack delivered the eulogy and said, "She was one of the beautiful people, the larger-than-life people who filled the screen."

Anita Louise was a child performer whose blonde beauty brought her fame as an adult film star in the 1930s and 1940s. She was born Anita Louise Fremault in New York City in 1917 and as a

Frank Lovejoy (1914–1962)

Frank Lovejoy was born in the Bronx on March 28, 1914. He acted with little theater groups and made his Broadway debut in *Judgment Day* in 1934. Other Broadway shows included *Pursuit of Happiness, Snark was a Boojum, Sound of Hunting,* and *Woman Bites Dog.*

When radio was in its heyday he gained great popularity as he appeared in more than 5000 radio broadcasts, including many soap operas. He was the narrator on "This Is Your FBI," Mr. Malone on "The Amazing Mr. Malone" and "Murder and Mr. Malone" and Lucky Stone in "Night Beat." Other shows included "Blue Playhouse," "Brave Tomorrow," "Bright Horizon," "Calling All Detectives," "Deadline Drama," "Gangbusters," "Gay Nineties Revue," "Joyce Jordan, Girl Intern," "The Man Behind the Gun," "Mr. District Attorney," "Stella Dallas," and many others.

Later he appeared on television in the series "Meet McGraw."

He made his motion picture debut in *Home of the Brave* for United Artists in 1949. Other films included, *Three Secrets, Breakthrough, Try and Get Me, Force of Arms, I Was a Communist for the F.B.I., Goodbye My Fancy, I'll See You in My Dreams, Retreat Hell!, Winning Team, House of Wax, Beachhead,* and *Charge at Feather River.*

He was twice married, his first wife being Frances Williams, a featured singer in the Billy Rose's Aquacade at the 1939 N. Y. World's Fair. His second wife was actress Joan Banks. His last professional appearance was in the play *The Best Man* at the Jersey theater. He died of a heart attack at the Warwick Hotel in New York City October 2, 1962.

Frank Lovejoy with Mari Blanchard and Richard Denning in The Crooked Web *(Columbia, 1955).*

Edmund Lowe with Betty Furness, Tala Birell, Ann Sothern, and Miriam Jordan in Let's Fall in Love *(Columbia, 1933).*

Edmund Lowe (1892–1971)

Edmund Lowe was one of the screen's most versatile leading men. During the silent film days of the 1920s, his gleaming black hair plastered tightly against his skull, his black mustache perfectly waxed, and his impeccable suavity, along with his husky athletic build, made him an idol for millions. He starred in almost a hundred movies, mostly as a dandy, but he is best remembered for his role as the hard-drinking, combat-wise Sergeant Quirt in the 1926 silent *What Price Glory?*, which teamed him with Victor McLaglen, who played Captain Flagg.

Born in San Jose, California, March 3, 1892, he was one of 13 children. His Irish mother named him for Edmund Dantes, the hero of Alexander Dumas' *The Count of Monte Cristo.* His father was a lawyer and a judge. He graduated from Santa Clara University at the age of 18, and later received a master's degree in pedagogy. Lowe launched his acting career in 1911 with Oliver Morosco's stock company in San Francisco. In 1917, he made his Broadway debut in *The Brat,* and after a series of plays came to Hollywood in 1923 under contract to Fox Films, where two of his initial films were *The Silent Command* and *Vive La France.*

But it was his characterization of Sergeant Quirt that gave him his enduring stature, and started a genre with actors better at such roles than he. Yet he was known for his suavity both on the screen and in his personal life, and next to Adolph Menjou he was regarded as probably the best-dressed actor in movies. Some of his film credits included *Cockeyed World, Call Out the Marines, Wings of the Eagle, Dinner at Eight, The Misleading Lady,* and *I Love That Man.* His final screen appearance was in *Heller in Pink Tights* in 1960. He died at the Motion Picture County House on April 21, 1971, after nearly twenty years of failing health.

Diana Lynn (1926–1971)

Diana Lynn starred in many light comedies in the 1940s. She broke into the movies as a musician at the age of thirteen. She was born Dolly Loehr on October 7, 1926, the daughter of a Los Angeles oil supply company executive. Her big break in movies came when she appeared as a teenager in *The Major and the Minor,* a 1942 wartime comedy starring Ray Milland and Ginger Rogers. Her favorable notices won more roles for her in *The Miracle of Morgan's Creek* and *Henry Aldrich Plays Cupid.* She appeared as a bandleader opposite Eddie Bracken in *Out of This World.* Miss Lynn achieved stardom in *Our Hearts Were Young and Gay* in 1944.

She did not forget an earlier childhood ambition, however, to be a concert pianist, and in 1943 she made her concert debut in Los Angeles. During World War II, she played many benefit concerts and in 1946 she produced a classical record album. She made her stage debut as Hedvig in Ibsen's *The Wild Duck* at the City Center in New York in 1956. She also made a number of television appearances over the years.

Her movie appearances also included *There's Magic in Music, Our Hearts Were Growing Up, Ruthless, Variety Girl, My Friend Irma, Peggy, Meet Me at the Fair, You're Never Too Young, The Kentuckian,* and *Annapolis Story.* In 1971, after more than 15 years, she was returning to the movies in Joan Didion's *Play It as It Lays.* Miss Lynn died in December, 1971, in Los Angeles after having suffered a stroke.

Diana Lynn with Barry Fitzgerald in Easy Come, Easy Go *(Paramount, 1946).*

Herbert Marshall (1890–1966)

Herbert Marshall was one of the most successful members of the "English colony" in Hollywood for decades. The urbane manner of the British gentleman was his trademark as an actor.

He was born in London on May 23, 1890, to parents both of whom were actors, and began his career in 1911 as a stage manager and with walk-on parts. He served in the British Expeditionary Forces during World War I, in which he was seriously wounded and had to have his leg amputated. The war injury came when Marshall was with the 14th London Scots Regiment, in which Ronald Colman also served. He learned to manage mobility on the stage and on the studio floor, though directors had to plan crosses with the dis-ability in mind.

He was a leading man in appearances in silent and talking pictures to such stars as Pauline Frederick, Jeanne Eagels, Greta Garbo, and Claudette Colbert. Some of his best performances were given in *Blonde Venus, Foreign Correspondent, The Little Foxes, The Moon and Sixpence, The Razor's Edge, The Enchanted Cottage,* and *Duel in the Sun.* Marshall was married five times and his daughter Sarah Best Marshall appeared in many Broadway stage plays. In recent years Marshall was active in various films. He collapsed and died of a heart attack at his Beverly Hills home on January 22, 1966.

Herbert Marshall with Keye Luke in **Painted Veil** *(MGM, 1935).*

*Marilyn Maxwell with Jerry Lewis and Connie Stevens
in* Rock-A-Bye Baby *(Paramount, 1958).*

Marilyn Maxwell (1921–1972)

Marilyn Maxwell starred in numerous song-and-dance movies during the 1940s and typified the durable blonde with a breezy manner.

She was born in Clarinda, Iowa, on August 3, 1921, and made her debut as a singer at the Brandeis Theatre in Omaha. She became a band singer, and in 1937 she joined Buddy Rogers' band and later worked with the Ted Weems' Orchestra. She was at the Pasadena Playhouse in 1941 and began to appear in films as a singer and actress during World War II. She appeared with Robert Taylor in *Stand By for Action,* with Wallace Beery in *Salute to the Marines,* with Kay Kyser in *Swing Fever,* and Abbott and Costello in *Lost in the Harem.* She also appeared with Van Johnson in several Dr. Kildare films. In 1948, she won critical praise for her role as Belle in *Summer Holiday,* a musical screen version of Eugene O'Neill's *Ah! Wilderness.*

Miss Maxwell toured with Bob Hope during the Korean War and also worked in top nightclubs such as the Latin Quarter in New York. She appeared on television's "Bus Stop" series in 1961 and in recent years made frequent guest appearances on "Password," "Talent Scout," "Play Your Hunch," and "The Red Skelton Show." Her other films included *Presenting Lily Mars, Thousands Cheer, High Barbaree, Key to the City, Champion, Off Limits, Critic's Choice, The Lively Set,* and *Arizona Bushwhackers.* On March 20, 1972, she died of a pulmonary ailment in her Beverly Hills home.

75

Joel McCrea with Virginia Mayo in **The Tall Stranger**
(Allied Artists, 1957).

Joel McCrea (1905–   )

Joel McCrea was born in Los Angeles, California, on November 5, 1905. He attended Pomona College and received early stage experience in community plays and amateur dramatics, and had the male lead in *The Little Journey, The Patsy,* and *Laff that Off.* In the early 1920s he became a stunt man and extra, and sometimes his duties were just holding the horses of William S. Hart and Tom Mix.

Although today he is more closely identified with his western roles, he has appeared in many other type films particularly in his early film years. He got his start in 1929 and appeared in *Jazz Age, Five O'Clock Girl, So This is College, The Single Standard,* and *Dynamite.* It was while playing in *Dynamite* that he struck up a lasting friendship with Cecil B. DeMille.

The likable McCrea projected the average man image and began to appear in many drawing-room dramas. His films included *Kept Husbands, Born to Love, Most Dangerous Game, Bed of Roses, Gambling Lady, Half a Sinner, Woman Chases Man, Dead End, Espionage Agent, Foreign Correspondent, Sullivan's Travels,* and *The More the Merrier.* His western films include *Silver Horde, Wells Fargo, Union Pacific, Buffalo Bill, The Virginian, Colorado Territory, The Outriders, Saddle Tramp, Cattle Drive, Wichita, Trooper Hook, The Tall Stranger,* and *Ride the High Country.*

In his early Hollywood days be became the constant companion of Constance Bennett, but on October 20, 1933 he married actress Frances Dee. They had three sons—one, Jody, also is pursuing an acting career. In 1952, along with Charles Boyer, Dick Powell, and Rosalind Russell they formed the popular "Four Star Playhouse" on television. In 1959, he and Jody starred in the western series "Wichita Town" on television.

Joel McCrea has long been interested in ranching and horses, and he and his wife have enjoyed ranch life for many years. He has also been very successful in real estate ventures; this has made him wealthy.

Marie McDonald (1923–1965)

Marie MacDonald was tagged "The Body" by enterprising press agents in a Hollywood career that was marked by sensational headlines. Born Marie Frye in Burgin, Kentucky, on July 6, 1923, she started her professional career as a John Power model in New York, then turned to the theater to appear in *George White's Scandals* in 1939.

Prior to coming to Hollywood in 1941, where her first picture was Universal's *It Started With Eve,* she was the vocalist for Tommy Dorsey's band. Following several pictures at Universal, which included *You're Telling Me* and *Pardon My Sarong,* she signed a contract at Paramount, where she was dubbed "The Body." She appeared at Paramount with Alan Ladd in *Lucky Jordan,* then Hunt Stromberg borrowed her for a featured role in his *Guest in the House.*

In 1957, a wide search was begun for Miss McDonald who claimed later that she had been kidnapped. She was married seven times to six men, twice to millionaire shoe manufacturer Harry Karl. Her other films included *It Started With Eve, Hit Parade of 1951, Swell Guy, Living in a Big Way, Tell It to the Judge,* and her last film, in 1963, *Promises, Promises.* In the late 1950s she became a top supper-club attraction, using the vocal talents that Hollywood never capitalized on. On October 21, 1965, she was found dead from an apparent overdose of drugs.

Marie McDonald with Dennis O'Keefe, Barry Sullivan, and Jerome Cowan in **Getting Gertie's Garter** *(United Artists, 1945).*

Ann Miller (1919–   )

Ann Miller was born Lucille Ann Collier on April 12, 1919, in Chireno, Texas. Her father was an attorney. She took up dancing at the age of three to improve her health, and to satisfy her mother who had high hopes for her daughter. They came to Hollywood when she was 13 although nothing much happened. She played the West Coast vaudeville houses and finally got a screen test with RKO. She signed a contract and had a tap dance specialty number in *New Faces of 1937* that year.

She made several films for RKO including *Stage Door, Life of the Party, Radio City Revels, Room Service, Tarnished Angel,* and *Having a Wonderful Time,* all in 1937 and 1938. She also landed a part in the Academy Award-winning film, *You Can't Take It With You,* for Columbia in 1938. She left RKO and appeared on Broadway in the 1940 edition of *George White's Scandals.*

Upon her return to Hollywood she made films for RKO, Republic, Columbia, and Paramount, and signed with Columbia appearing in *Reveille With Beverly, What's Buzzin', Cousin?, Jam Ses-* *sion, Hey Rookie, Carolina Blues, Eve Knew Her Apples, Eadie Was a Lady,* and *Thrill of Brazil.*

In 1947 she signed with MGM and her first film for them was *The Kissing Bandit* in 1948, which turned out to be a very poor film. Better things were to come, however, as her appearance in many MGM musicals added much to their films in the late forties and fifties. She appeared in *Easter Parade, On the Town, Texas Carnival, Lovely to Look At, Kiss Me, Kate!, Small Town Girl, Deep in My Heart, Hit the Deck, The Opposite Sex,* and her last film *The Great American Pastime* in 1956.

She left Hollywood, went on the road, and appeared in such shows as *Can Can, Glad Tidings, Mame,* and *Hello, Dolly.* Television viewers were treated to one of the cleverest commercials in years when she tap danced in the Great American Soup's commercial in 1971. She also appeared in a TV special the same year, *Dames At Sea,* with Ann-Margret, and the result of both TV appearances proved she certainly still has what it takes to be a top-flight personality.

Ann Miller with Red Skelton in Watch the Birdie
(MGM, 1950).

Carmen Miranda with Louis Calhern in **Nancy Goes to Rio** *(MGM, 1950).*

Carmen Miranda (1909–1955)

Carmen Miranda was born Maria do Carmo Miranda da Cunha in Marco de Canavezes, Portugal, on February 9, 1909. She was taken to Rio de Janeiro, Brazil, three months later by her father who began a produce business there.

She was educated in the Convent of Saint Teresenha. She later went to work in a local store and then landed a job as a singer on a local radio show. By 1928, her style had been widely accepted in South America. She switched to nightclubs and in 1935 started appearing in musical comedy films in Brazil.

By 1939 she had made 300 records, which later sold like hot cakes in North America. She continued her night club work and was spotted by Lee Shubert, and he signed her to an exclusive contract and she appeared in his Broadway production of *Streets of Paris* in 1939. She was an instant smash. She continued her night club rounds only this time in the U.S.A. and was introduced to radio by Rudy Vallee on the "Rudy Vallee Show."

In 1940, Darryl F. Zanuck signed her for 20th Century-Fox to appear with Betty Grable and Don Ameche in *Down Argentine Way*. This was a success with the critics and the audiences and she then made *That Night in Rio, Weekend in Havana, Springtime in the Rockies, The Gang's All Here,*

Four Jills in a Jeep, Greenwich Village, Something for the Boys, Doll Face, and *If I'm Lucky* all for 20th Century-Fox. She appeared in *Copacabana* for United Artists, *A Date With Judy* and *Nancy Goes to Rio* for MGM, and her last film *Scared Stiff* for Paramount in 1953.

She continued her performances in nightclubs and tours. On August 4, 1955, she taped a half-hour show with Jimmy Durante, there was an impromptu party afterwards, and in the early hours of the next morning she collapsed and died of a heart attack. She had been under treatment for bronchitis following her return from an engagement at the Tropicana Club in Havana.

The Brazilian bombshell was certainly one of a kind. Her explosive style of acting and singing has only been imitated, never equalled. Her own brand of moving around, rapid speech, wearing apparel that included more costume jewelry than you can find at the dime store, and her turbans of artificial fruit as she moved about singing "South American Way," "The Nango," "Chica, Chica, Boom, Chic," "I Yi, Yi, Yi," "Thank You North America," and "Ay, Ay, Ay" can now only be found if you happen to catch one of her films on television.

Maria Montez with Jon Hall in White Savage Woman
(Universal, 1943).

Maria Montez (1920–1951)

Maria Montez is best remembered for her half-dozen films with Jon Hall. She was noted for her siren portrayals and was known as the "Queen of Technicolor" during the World War II years when she made more than twenty pictures for Universal, and was one of that studio's biggest money-makers.

Miss Montez was born on June 6, 1920, in the Dominican Republic, of Spanish parents. Her father was the Spanish consul. She was brought up with a strict convent education and traveled a great deal throughout Europe. She married a British army officer at 17 and remained in the United States after divorcing her husband. She was introduced into café society and in 1940 she was given a Universal contract at $150 per week.

She remained under contract until 1948. Her first film was *Boss of Bullion City* but her appearance in a second film, *The Invisible Woman*, was released first. Her other films included *That Night in Rio, Moonlight in Hawaii, South of Tahiti, Bombay Clipper, Arabian Nights, Ali Baba and the Forty Thieves, Follow the Boys, Cobra Woman, Sudan, Tangier, Pirates of Monterey,* and *Siren of Atlantis.*

In 1943 she married French actor, Jean Pierre Aumont. In addition to her American films, she made a number of French and Italian pictures. Her last film, *Sensuality,* was made in Rome. She died unexpectedly on September 7, 1951, of a heart attack, in her bath.

Dennis Morgan (1910–   )

Dennis Morgan was born Stanley Morner on December 20, 1910, in Prentice, Wisconsin. His father was a lumberman and banker in that community. He attended the local schools and the 6′2″ Morgan played basketball, football, baseball, and participated in track. He left home for the University of Wisconsin and then attended and graduated from Carroll College at Waukeska. During this time he kept in shape by working out as a lumberjack at his father's camps.

After college he got a job as a radio announcer and singer in Milwaukee. He did a little stock, continued his musical studies at several conservatories and played semiprofessional baseball in the Northern Wisconsin League. He appeared with the State Lake Theatre in Chicago and toured the Midwest in *Faust*. He also sang at the Empire Room of the Palmer House in Chicago and appeared on NBC radio programs.

His first film was a small role in *I Conquer the Sun* in early 1936 for Academy Pictures. The real start of his career began when Mary Garden, the opera star, heard him sing and persuaded MGM to sign him on. He had several minor roles and used his real name of Stanley Morner. Allan Jones even dubbed his singing voice in one film. He was then signed by Paramount and changed his name to Richard Stanley. It was still not the break he had been hoping for. He was ready to give it up when Producer Charles Rogers saw and heard him and signed him at Warner Bros. His name was changed to Dennis Morgan.

With the exception of being loaned to RKO for a dramatic role in *Kitty Foyle* in 1940, all of his films were for Warner Bros. from 1939 to 1952. *The Desert Song* in 1943 gave fans their first opportunity to hear the Morgan voice.

His films included *Waterfront, The Fighting 69th, Bad Men of Missouri, Captains of the Clouds, Wings for the Eagle, The Very Thought of You, Shine on Harvest Moon, God is My Co-Pilot, Christmas in Connecticut, Two Guys From Milwaukee, My Wild Irish Rose, One Sunday Afternoon, Perfect Strangers, Pretty Baby,* and *Cattle Town.* His last film was *Rogue's Gallery* in 1968 for Paramount, and this was after a layoff of 12 years.

In 1959 he starred on television as a private eye in "21 Beacon Street."

Dennis Morgan with Roy Gordon in **The Gun That Won the West** *(Columbia, 1955).*

Chester Morris (1901–1970)

Chester Morris was born Manchester Morris on February 16, 1901, the son of William Morris, a prominent actor, and Etta Hawkins, an outstanding comedienne in the Charles Frohman era. He dropped out of school at an early age and toured the country with his family. For two years they played in a sketch called *All the Horrors of Home* written by his father. At the age of 12 he made his debut as a magician billed as *The Mysterious Morris*. His brothers and his sister were also in show business with brother, Adrian, becoming a character actor in many films.

He received his early stage training with the Westchester Players after graduating from the New York School of Fine Arts. He went to see a New York theatrical agent and the agent sent him to see Augustus Thomas, playwright, who was about to stage *The Copperhead*. He made his Broadway debut in *The Copperhead* in 1918 in support of Lionel Barrymore. In the play he played a 35-year-old man. He was seen in several New York productions after that. He joined George M. Cohan's company for a five-year stay as a contract player and was then signed by D. W. Griffith in 1928. Griffith turned Chester down for a leading man in a new picture and Roland West asked Griffith if he could have Morris to play in *Alibi*. Griffith said "Yes."

He made his talking film debut in *Alibi* in 1929 and was nominated for an Oscar, losing to Warner Baxter for his role in *In Old Arizona*. He played a series of gangster roles after *Alibi* and some of his films included *The Big House, Cock of the Air, Blondie Johnson, Divorcee, Gift of Gab, Public Hero No. 1, They Met In A Taxi, Pacific Liner, Five Came Back, High Explosive, Aerial Gunner, Secret Command, Unchained,* and *The Great White Hope.*

He probably gained his greatest fame as *Boston Blackie* from 1941 through 1950 in 13 Boston Blackie films for Columbia. He was the wise-cracking, girl-chasing former jewel thief turned good guy and was perfect for the part. In the pictures he had a dull-witted partner called Runt and was constantly being harassed by Inspector Farraday as he solved the crimes in each adventure. Morris also played the role on radio, which began as a summer replacement for "Amos 'n' Andy."

During World War II, Morris made more than 380 USO appearances for the troops, showing off his abilities as a magician. He made few film appearances after 1949. He toured in *Detective Story* and was seen on Broadway in *The Fifth Season, Blue Denim, Advise and Consent,* and *The Subject was Roses.* He also made many television appearances.

He died of an overdose of barbiturates on September 11, 1970, in New Hope, Pennsylvania, where he was appearing at the Bucks County Playhouse as Captain Queeg in *The Caine Mutiny Court-Martial.*

Chester Morris with Luis Van Rooten, Joan Wood-
bury, and George Lloyd in Boston Blackie's Chinese
Adventure *(Columbia, 1949).*

Wayne Morris with Ida Lupino in Deep Valley *(Warner Bros., 1947).*

Wayne Morris (1914–1959)

Wayne Morris was born Bert de Wayne Morris in Los Angeles on February 17, 1914. He attended Los Angeles City College where he won a scholarship to the Pasadena Playhouse. He appeared in his first film in 1936 entitled *China Clipper* for First National. This was followed by other supporting roles the same year in *Here Comes Carter!* and *King of Hockey.* A Warner Bros. talent scout who was looking for an athletic type to play the lead in *Kid Galahad* signed him for the title role. *Kid Galahad* was released in 1937, and this made him an overnight sensation and they signed him to a long-term contract. Other films that he appeared in were *Men Are Such Fools, Valley of the Giants, Brother Rat, The Kid from Kokomo, Brother Rat and a Baby, Double Alibi, Ladies Must Live, The Quarterback, I Wanted Wings, Bad Men of Missouri,* and *The Smiling Ghost.*

World War II erupted and he was one of the first to leave Hollywood for military duty. He spent five years in the Navy and was discharged a lieutenant commander. He was truly a war hero in the true sense of the word. He was based on the famous aircraft carrier Essex and took part in the raids on Iwo Jima, Okinawa, Wake, and Marcus. He was credited with shooting down seven Japanese aircraft in aerial dogfights, sinking a Japanese gunboat and two enemy destroyers, and helping to destroy a submarine. He was awarded four Distinguished Flying Crosses and two air medals.

Upon his return to Hollywood he appeared in *Voice of the Turtle* and *Deep Valley,* and appeared in many westerns including *The Younger Brothers, Stage to Tucson, Star of Texas, The Fighting Lawman,* and *Riding Shotgun.* His career in films was not so spectacular as before the war. He starred on the stage in the touring companies of *The Tender Trap* and *Mr. Roberts.* He made his Broadway debut in the 1957 William Saroyan comedy *The Cave Dwellers.* His film career had him working for Allied Artists and he then went to England where he free-lanced.

On September 14, 1959, he was visiting his wartime squadron leader aboard the U.S. aircraft carrier *Bon Homme Richard* docked at Oakland, California. He suffered a fatal heart attack while watching the aerial maneuvers.

Jean Muir (1911-   )

Jean Muir was born Jean Muir Fullarton, February 13, 1911 in New York City. Her Scottish father was an importer of spices with an Indian importing company and her mother was a manual training teacher. The family moved to Ridgewood, New Jersey, shortly thereafter where she lived until she was 16.

When she was nine years old she saw *The Merchant of Venice* with Ethel Barrymore and Walter Hampden and from that moment on she knew she wanted to be an actress. She learned the role of Portia in only four days. She kept reading about acting and in high school she performed in the local plays. She had planned to go to college, but was sent to Scotland by her father to meet her relatives. She journeyed to France in 1930 and studied in a Paris conservatory. The "crash" caused her father to bring her home and she landed a role as an understudy in a Shubert touring company in John Drinkwater's *Bird In Hand*. She got her big chance to appear on the stage when the leading lady had other commitments.

During the depression Hollywood came to New York and raided every ingenue. She went along with Katharine Hepburn, Jean Arthur, Margaret Sullivan, and Jane Wyatt. She was down to her last $20.00. She decided to only go for six months, but Hal Wallis starred her immediately. The studio wanted to change her name to Jean Fullar, but she balked and they settled for Jean Muir. She was under contract to Warner Brothers and appeared in such films as *As the Earth Turns, Gentlemen Are Born, Bedside, A Modern Hero, The White Cockatoo, Oil For the Lamps of China, Stars Over Broadway, Draegerman Courage, Fugitive in the Sky, Her Husband's Secretary, Once A Doctor, White Bondage,* and *Dance, Charlie, Dance.* For Fox she appeared in *Orchids to You* and *White Fang.*

In 1937 the studio did not pick up her option.

By her own admission she was somewhat of a rebel, had high principles, disliked Hollywood and wanted to return to the stage. By then she was undisciplined for the stage and she returned to Hollywood in 1940 to do *And One Was Beautiful* for MGM. It was the same year of her marriage to attorney Henri Jaffe. She followed her husband who was in the service during World War II but did make one film in 1943, *The Constant Nymph,* for Warner Brothers.

In 1950 she was signed for a television show but one-and-a-half hours before going on the air her appearance was questioned due to her activities many years before. In 1936, she joined an organization that she thought was in support of President Roosevelt and this led to her being blacklisted due to alleged communistic affiliations.

The years 1950 to 1959 are blank for her because of her alcoholism. She did have a comeback in 1960 as she appeared on television and back on Broadway. She moved to Westchester, a suburb of New York and directed plays. In 1968 she moved to Columbia, Missouri, where she became a master acting teacher at Stephens College.

Her favorite film was *Desirable* for sentimental reasons. It was her first so-called starring role and the story was similar to her own life. Her favorite director was Mervyn LeRoy. She feels Hollywood in the 1930s was absolutely wild with the almighty dollar as the only thing. She just could not adjust to the situation. As far as her friends during that era are concerned, Joan Crawford was one, and she felt that James Cagney was a real gentleman with a wealth of knowledge and considered him as her closest friend.

Today she resides in Columbia, Missouri, living quietly with her boxer, "Taffy." She plans for and directs the freshman drama students at Stephens College. As far as current movies are concerned, she feels they are better than ever.

Jean Muir with Michael Whalen in White Fang
(20th Century-Fox, 1936).

Tom Neal with Ann Savage in Detour *(PRC, 1946).*

Tom Neal (1914–1972)

Tom Neal played he-man roles in more than a hundred "B" films during the 1940s and early 1950s. He played in films such as *Another Thin Man, Behind the Rising Sun, The Flying Tigers, First Yank Into Tokyo, The Hat Box Mystery,* and *Call of the Klondike.* Neal's acting career, which achieved some prominence in the 1940s, faded somewhat after he broke Franchot Tone's nose in a celebrated fistfight over the affections of blonde actress Barbara Payton. In later years Neal operated a landscaping firm.

In April, 1965, the body of his wife, Gail, was found in their Palm Springs home on a divan, shot through the head. Neal was convicted of involuntary manslaughter after a sensational four-week trial in which the prosecution charged that he shot his estranged wife while she slept. He contended that she was shot accidentally after an attempt at a reconciliation. The jury took two days to reach a verdict. Neal served his sentence at the California Institution for Men at Chino and was paroled in December, 1971. On August 7, 1972, he died.

Lloyd Nolan (1903–   )

Lloyd Nolan was born August 11, 1903, in San Francisco. He received his education at the Santa Clara Preparatory school and spent a year at Stanford University. He then went to sea and worked his way around the world. His seamanship was distinguished by running a tramp steamer into the rocks at Marseilles. He then resumed his studies at Stanford.

His first theatrical experience was when he joined the Pasadena Community Playhouse in 1927. He then worked for Edward Everett Horton in *Queen's Husband* at his repertory theatre. This performance enabled him to understudy Roger Pryor who had the lead in *Front Page*. From there he worked at the famous Dennis Theatre at Cape Cod as a stagehand. He played in stock with Helen Hayes and Pat O'Brien in *Sweet Stranger* in New York. Also, a member of the cast was Mel Efrid, who became his wife in 1933.

Other stage appearances included *High Hat* with Edna Hibbard, *Reunion in Vienna* with Fontanne and Lunt and *Americana, One Sunday Afternoon,* and *Ragged Army.* In 1934 he went to Hollywood under contract to Paramount and appeared in a variety of roles from the handsome hero to the guiltless "heavy." His first film was *Stolen Harmony* in 1935.

His other films include *G-Men, The Texas Rangers, Wells Fargo, King of Alcatraz, Johnny Apollo, Michael Shayne, Private Detective, Mr. Dynamite, Manila Calling, Bataan, Guadalcanal Diary, A Tree Grows In Brooklyn, The House on 92nd Street, Peyton Place, Circus World, Never Too Late,* and *Ice Station Zebra.*

***Lloyd Nolan** with Claire Trevor in* **King of Gamblers** *(Paramount, 1937).*

Jack Oakie with Binnie Barnes in **Thanks for Every-thing** *(20th Century-Fox, 1938).*

Jack Oakie (1903–   )

Jack Oakie was long considered one of the screen's most notorious scene stealers. He had a unique brand of comedy and was the master of the double and triple take.

He was born Lewis Delaney Offield on November 12, 1903, in Sedalia, Missouri. His father was a grain dealer and his mother was a psychology teacher. Oakie got his stage surname from the move that his family made to Muskogee, Oklahoma, when he was five. In the 1920s he landed a job as a dancer in George M. Cohan's *Little Nelly Kelly* on Broadway. He went from Broadway to vaudeville with Lulu McConnell as his partner, before roles in *Artists and Models, Innocent Eyes,* and others.

In 1927, Oakie went to Hollywood and in his first film he was cast as a comedian in Director Wesley Ruggles's *Finders Keepers.* He was under contract to Paramount for nine years where he played the perennial freshman at "Paramount U."

He appeared in many of the big musicals of the day with Bing Crosby, Lanny Ross, Lily Pons, Burns and Allen, Maurice Chevalier, and Alice Faye all making their first pictures with the cherubic Oakie in the cast.

His characterization of Benito Mussolini in Charlie Chaplin's *Great Dictator* won him a supporting actor's nomination for an Oscar in 1940. His pictures included *Chinatown Nights, Paramount on Parade, Touchdown, Once in a Lifetime, Sailor Be Good, College Rhythm, Call of the Wild, Big Broadcast of 1936, Thanks for Everything, Hello, Frisco, Hello, The Merry Monahans, When My Baby Smiles at Me, Around the World in 80 Days,* and *Lover Come Back.* In recent years he has made some television appearances and lives in baronial style on a ten-acre estate in Northridge, at the northern end of the San Fernando Valley.

Dennis O'Keefe with Tommye Adams in **Tahiti Honey** *(Republic, 1943).*

Dennis O'Keefe (1908–1968)

Dennis O'Keefe's light-hearted screen personality was not forced. He was the same off screen. Tall, husky, and blond, he was during the 1930s and 1940s one of the movie industry's busiest performers. He was born Edward Vanes Flanagan, Jr. on March 29, 1908, in Fort Madison, Iowa, the son of vaudeville performers known on the circuits as "Flanagan and Edwards, The Rollicking Twosome." The family went to Hollywood in 1918.

At the age of sixteen, O'Keefe was writing scripts for the "Our Gang" comedies. He attended the University of Southern California but dropped out to go into vaudeville. He returned to Hollywood and worked for the studios in various jobs as extra and stuntman. Clark Gable noticed him as an extra in *Saratoga* in 1937 and he was given a screen test, was signed as a contract player by MGM, and his name was changed. Among the pictures that followed were *Topper*

Returns, Hold That Kiss, Unexpected Father, Affairs of Jimmy Valentine, Abroad with Two Yanks, The Story of Dr. Wassel, Sensations of 1945, Affairs of Susan, Brewster's Millions, Earl Carroll Vanities, and *Doll Face.*

After World War II he turned more toward action roles, usually as a sleuth in crime pictures like *T-Men, Raw Deal, Walk a Crooked Mile, Cover Up, Chicago Syndicate, Las Vegas Shakedown,* and *Inside Detroit.* He directed as well as starred in *The Diamond Wizard* and *Angela* and wrote scripts under his pen name, Jonathan Ricks. He also toured in the national company of *The Subject Was Roses.*

In 1958 he starred in a television series, "The Dennis O'Keefe Show," which was shortlived. He was married for many years to actress Steffi Duna. In October, 1967, O'Keefe was operated on for lung cancer at the Mayo Clinic in Rochester, Minnesota, and on August 31, 1968, he died.

Eleanor Parker (1922–   )

Eleanor Parker was born June 26, 1922, in Cedarville, Ohio, the daughter of a local high school teacher. She became interested in acting at a very early age, but it was not until her family moved to Cleveland that she had an opportunity to express herself. With her parents consent she joined a theater group. In 1941 she joined the players at the Pasadena Playhouse. Later that year she signed a Warner Bros. contract.

Warners promptly put the very beautiful Parker in *They Died With Their Boots On,* but due to the length of the film her part was cut out. Her first real screen appearance was in *Busses Roar* in 1942. Other Warner Bros. vehicles were *Mission to Moscow, Crime by Night, The Last Ride, The Very Thought of You, Pride of the Marines, Of Human Bondage, Never Say Goodbye, Escape Me Never, The Voice of the Turtle, Caged, Three Secrets,* and *Chain Lightning.* She then made *Valentino* for Columbia, *A Millionaire for Christy* for 20th Century-Fox, *The Detective Story* for Paramount, and then signed an MGM contract. Other films included *Scaramouche, Escape From Ft. Bravo, The Naked Jungle, Valley of Kings, The Man With the Golden Arm, The King and Four Queens, Home From the Hill, Return to Peyton Place, The Sound of Music,* and *Eye of the Cat.*

She was nominated for the Academy Award three times: for her portrayal as a prison inmate in *Caged* in 1950, for her role as a policeman's wife in *Detective Story* in 1951, and for her role as an opera star in *Interrupted Melody* in 1955.

She has done some television, including a regular part on "Bracken's World" in 1969, but when not appearing in films prefers to spend her free time with her family. It is nice to learn that the beautiful, aloof appearing star has the reputation of being very cooperative, a quick study, and one who does not give her directors headaches during the filming of a picture.

Eleanor Parker with Anthony Dexter in Valentino
(Columbia, 1951).

Jean Parker (1915–   )

Jean Parker was born Lois Mae Green on August 11, 1915, in Butte, Montana although most reference books list her birthplace as Deer Lodge, Montana. Her family moved to Pasadena, California, when she was a small child. While she was attending the John Muir High School in Pasadena she played in the school orchestra. The students in the school had an opportunity to enter a poster contest for the 1932 Olympic games held in Los Angeles. She was a 1st prize winner and was signed to an MGM contract. Her first film *Divorce in the Family* was released the same year when she was only 17. She then appeared as the little Duchess Maria with the Barrymores in *Rasputin and the Empress* also in 1932.

She appeared in several MGM films the following year including *Secret of Madame Blanche, Gabriel Over the White House, Made On Broadway,* and *Storm at Daybreak.* Her most exciting roles during this year were while on loan-out to RKO in *Little Women* and Columbia's *What Price Innocence.* She also graduated from high school in 1933 and was quite a celebrity in the graduating class.

The very beautiful, demure Parker did not lack for exposure throughout the rest of the 30s as she continually graced the screen at MGM including *Sequoia,* where the real star was a puma and the beautiful scenery. She was also opposite Fred MacMurray in *The Texas Rangers* in 1936. She moved to Columbia and although she obtained steady work it was mostly in "B" films and she also appeared in several films for Monogram and Republic.

Starting in 1941 she became the leading lady for Pine-Thomas unit for Paramount in their action films. She appeared opposite either Richard Arlen or Chester Morris in *Power Dive, Flying Blind, No Hands On the Clock, Torpedo Boat, I Live On Danger, Wrecking Crew, Alaska Highway, Minesweeper,* and *High Explosive* in this series of films. She also played an amateur sleuth in *Detective Kitty O'Day* and *The Adventures of Kitty O'Day* for Monogram.

She then took a stab at summer stock starring in *Candlelight, Guest in the House,* and *Berkeley Square.* She appeared on Broadway in *Loco* and *Burlesque* and was with the road company of *Dream Girl* and *Born Yesterday.*

She returned to films in 1950 in *The Gunfighter* opposite Gregory Peck and this led to a succession of hard-boiled roles as in *The Redheads From Seattle, Black Tuesday,* and *The Parson and the Outlaw.*

In 1936 she married New York newsman George MacDonald. They were divorced in 1940. She then married radio commentator Douglas Dawson in 1941. They were divorced and she married an insurance broker. This marriage did not last, and in 1951 she married actor Robert Lowery. They were divorced in 1957. She has not returned to films since a small part in *Apache Uprising* in 1966.

Jean Parker with Russell Hayden in Knights of the
Range *(Paramount, 1940).*

Kane Richmond as the Shadow with George Chandler in **Behind the Mask** *(Monogram, 1946).*

Kane Richmond (1906–1973)

Kane Richmond was born Fred W. Bowditch in Minneapolis, Minnesota, on December 23, 1906. He graduated from the University of Minnesota and became a film salesman, booker, and theater manager in Minnesota. While on the West Coast on business for Columbia Studios in 1930 he tested for the role of an athletic actor who also made an attractive looking boxer. This was for Universal who were about to make their first "Leather Pusher" film. He got the part and made twelve two-reelers in this series.

Although he made many films and was the romantic lead in many, the good looking Richmond earned the stamp of "hero" in many of his films. In 1936 and 1937 he appeared in several action films with Frankie Darro for Ambassador Pictures. In 1942 Republic signed him to portray the comic strip hero *Spy Smasher* in a 12-chapter serial. He was ideal for the role. In 1944 he starred in the 15-chapter serial *Haunted Harbor* again for Republic. In 1945 he starred in *Jungle Raiders* for Columbia and assisted Joan Woodbury in *Brenda Starr, Reporter.* In 1947 he made his last serial *Brick Bradford* also for Columbia. In 1946 he portrayed the mysterious masked Shadow in three films, *The Shadow Returns, Behind the Mask,* and *The Missing Lady.*

Other films in which he appeared were *Huddle, Devil Tiger, Nancy Steele is Missing, Return of the Cisco Kid, Charlie Chan in Reno, Charlie Chan in Panama, Riders of the Purple Sage, Three Russian Girls, Bermuda Mystery, The Mighty McGurk, Black Gold,* and *Stage Struck.*

His last film was in 1948, and he left the film industry to become a manufacturer's representative in the fashion industry. He was married to former actress, Marion Burns. He died on March 22, 1973.

Cesar Romero (1907–   )

Cesar Romero was born in New York City on February 15, 1907. His father was president of the Wall Street exporting firm, The Augustine Fuller & Co., and his maternal grandfather was Jose Marti, the Cuban national hero, known as the martyr of Cuban independence from Spain.

Upon graduating from Collegiate School for Boys in New York in 1926 he started in show business as a ballroom team. His first dancing partner was the socially prominent Lisbeth Higgins, heiress to the Higgins India Ink fortune. They made their first professional engagement at the Park Central Roof in New York City. He danced for four years with various partners in vaudeville, night clubs, and musical comedy. In 1930 he played his first part in the leading role of road company of *Strictly Dishonorable* replacing Tullio Carminati. They toured the South, Midwest, and Canada.

In the next three years he appeared in *The Social Register* with Lenore Ulric, *Ten Minute Alibi* with Bert Lytell, *Spring in Autumn* with Blanche Yurka, and the George Kaufman-Edna Ferber play *Dinner at Eight*.

In April of 1934 he went to Hollywood and signed an MGM contract. He made many films including *The Thin Man, Clive of India, Cardinal Richelieu, Wee Willie Winkie, Tall, Dark and Handsome, Orchestra Wives, Captain of Castile, Julia Misbehaves, Vera Cruz, Oceans Eleven,* and *The Computer Wore Tennis Shoes.* In 1939 he replaced Warner Baxter as the Cisco Kid and appeared in the title role in six of these adventures, all for 20th Century-Fox. His favorite roles were as Tobey in *Show Them No Mercy* in 1935, Cortez in *Captain From Castile* in 1947, Duke Santos in *Oceans Eleven* in 1960 and The Joker in *Batman* in 1966.

He is one star who is definitely happy to have been a part of the Golden Years of the motion picture business. He feels honored having worked with the likes of William Powell, Myrna Loy, Carole Lombard, Marlene Dietrich, Barbara Stanwyck, Tyrone Power, and many others. Although he came close a couple of times, the suave, handsome Romero never married. He has, through the years become the top escort of stars and beautiful women to parties and premieres and he is still at it.

Cesar Romero with Paul Douglas, Sid Tomack, and Ed Max in Love That Brute *(20th Century-Fox, 1950).*

Gail Russell (1924–1961)

Gail Russell was a beautiful young actress whose life held many of the tragedies usually associated by audiences with female movie stars.

She was born in Chicago on September 23, 1924, and discovered by a Paramount talent scout while she was attending high school at Santa Monica, California. Her first film role was in 1943 in *Henry Aldrich Gets Glamour*. She was a very shy person thrust quickly into the Hollywood limelight when she was cast in support of Ginger Rogers in *Lady in the Dark* in 1944.

In her third film, she was cast in the ingenue lead opposite Ray Milland. She was married to actor Guy Madison in 1949 and divorced in 1954. Her personal shyness and humility gave her an essential sympathy on the screen and a withdrawn and tragic quality in real life. The actress who was a critics' selection for Star of Tomorrow in 1947, had a record of several arrests for drunken driving during the 1950s.

On August 27, 1961, her body was found on the living room floor of her West Los Angeles apartment. Police said that there was an empty vodka bottle near the body and several other empty vodka bottles in the kitchen and bedroom. Some of her other film credits included *Our Hearts Were Young and Gay, The Unseen, Salty O'-Rourke, Calcutta, Angel and the Bad Man* (probably her best performance), *Variety Girl, Wake of the Red Witch, Song of India, El Paso, Seven Men From Now,* and her last film *The Silent Call*.

Gail Russell with John Wayne in Wake of the Red Witch *(Republic, 1948).*

96

Sabu with Maria Montez and Constance Purdy in
White Savage Woman *(Universal, 1943).*

Sabu (1924–1963)

During his acting career Sabu was only known by his first name. He was born Sabu Dastagir in India in 1924. He was a discovery of director Robert Flaherty who cast him in Sir Alexander Korda's *Elephant Boy* in 1937. Sabu was the orphaned 12-year-old son of a mahout in the elephant stables of Maharajah of Mysore at the time Flaherty was casting the Rudyard Kipling story. His engaging personality and fearless talents in riding the elephants landed him the job over several other candidates. The picture was a success and made Sabu a well-known name almost overnight.

He returned to England with Flaherty and became a ward of the British Government. He attended one of the more aristocratic schools while continuing his career in the Denham studios. His second film was *Drums* in 1938, and his performance as Prince Azim was enthusiastically re-viewed. When he made his first visit to the United States to publicize the film he immediately became a hit with the reporters and all who came in contact with him.

He appeared in *The Thief of Bagdad* in 1940 and *The Jungle Book* in 1941. He then signed with Universal and made three spectaculars with Maria Montez and Jon Hall entitled *Arabian Nights*, *White Savage*, and *Cobra Woman*. He became a U.S. citizen and joined the U.S. Army Air Force where he earned the Distinguished Flying Cross. After his wartime service he returned to films and appeared in *Tangier, Black Narcissus, Song of India, Savage Drums, Jaguar, Rampage,* and *A Tiger Walks.*

He died of a heart attack December 2, 1963, and was survived by his widow, former actress Marilyn Cooper and two children.

Lizabeth Scott with Humphrey Bogart in Dead Reckoning *(Columbia, 1947).*

Lizabeth Scott (1922–   )

Lizabeth Scott was born Emma Matzo on September 29, 1922, in Scranton, Pennsylvania. She graduated from Central College there and attended Marywood College, a Catholic school near her home, for a short time. She went to Manhattan and enrolled at the Alvienne School of Dramatics and stayed there for one-and-a-half years.

In 1940 she joined the national company of *Hellzapoppin* for a season of hard work with one night stands in every state. When this was over she made the rounds of all the casting offices with no luck. She did land a job as a model for *Harper's Bazaar* and also posed for other magazines. She did get a job in stock as Sadie Thompson in *Rain*.

In 1942 she landed a job as Tallulah Bankhead's understudy in *The Skin of Our Teeth*. After many months of doing nothing she decided she wasn't getting anywhere and left the show. Bankhead was replaced by Miriam Hopkins. When Hopkins became ill one evening she was hastily called upon to play the part and did so for a few weeks. She then returned to modeling and had several screen tests that did not materialize. Hal Wallis reviewed one of her screen tests, liked what he saw, and awarded her a contract and she left for Hollywood in 1944.

Her first film was released in 1945 and she appeared with Bob Cummings, Don DeFore, and Charles Drake in *You Came Along*. Films that followed were *The Strange Love of Martha Ivers, Dead Reckoning, Desert Fury, I Walk Alone, Variety Girl, Pitfall, Too Late for Tears, Easy Living, Paid in Full, Dark City, The Racket, The Company She Keeps, Two of a Kind, Red Mountain, Stolen Face, Scared Stiff, Bad For Each Other, Silver Lode, Loving You,* and her last *The Weapon* in 1957. The sultry-voiced actress retired from films and recorded an album, spent a lot of time reading, enrolled in many college courses, made several commercials, and has been able to exist by wise investments made during her film career.

Zachary Scott (1914–1965)

In a screen career that spanned twenty-one years, Zachary Scott specialized in slick villainy and was noted as the smooth, tough, but charming heel—very attractive to women. Offscreen, he was considered one of the film industry's most charming personalities.

After dropping out of the University of Texas, where he headed the drama club, he worked his way to Europe on a freighter and began his professional acting career in London. He spent nearly two years with the English Repertory Company. After his return to the United States, he played summer stock before Broadway parts in *Ah, Wilderness, Damask Cheek,* and other plays. Jack Warner signed him to a film contract after seeing him in *Those Endearing Young Charms.*

Scott made his screen debut in 1943 in *The Mask of Dimitrios.* Other roles included his brilliant portrayal as a cad in *Mildred Pierce, Cass Timberlane, Appointment in Honduras, Her Kind of Man,* and *The Southerner,* in which he gave one of his finest performances for French director Rene Clair. He also appeared in *Born To Be Bad* and *The Young One* in 1961 for Luis Bunuel. After a long series of films in which he felt he was being typed, Scott returned to the theatre in 1956 for a revival of *The King and I,* and later *Requiem for a Nun* and *Rainy Day in Newark.*

His first marriage to Elaine Anderson ended in divorce in 1949 and in 1952 he married actress Ruth Ford. Scott became bedridden in July, following brain surgery in New York. On October 3, 1965, he died at his home in Austin, Texas, of a malignant brain tumor.

Zachary Scott with Joel McCrea and Nacho Galindo in South of St. Louis *(Warner Bros., 1949).*

99

Ann Sheridan (1915–1967)

Ann Sheridan was not only the "oomph girl" of the movies during the World War II years, but was one of Hollywood's outstanding young actresses.

She was born Clara Lou Sheridan on February 21, 1915, in Denton, Texas. After high school she studied at North Texas State Teachers College. Her sister submitted Miss Sheridan's photograph in a "Search for Beauty" contest conducted by Paramount studios, and she won a two-year contract and was cast in her first film, *Search for Beauty.*

At the expiration of this contract, she signed a contract with Warner Brothers where she became one of that studio's most versatile leading ladies, appearing opposite such stars as Humphrey Bogart, James Cagney, Errol Flynn, Cary Grant, Gary Cooper, and George Raft. Among her films were *The Crusades, Black Legion, Angels with Dirty Faces, Dodge City, King's Row, George Washington Slept Here, The Man Who Came to Dinner, Nora Prentiss, Shine on Harvest Moon, They Drive by Night, I Was a Male War Bride, Woman on the Run, Appointment in Honduras, Steel Town,* and probably her best performance, *Come Next Spring.*

Miss Sheridan also was active on the stage and television. At the time of her death in 1967, she was starring in a television series, "Pistols 'n' Petticoats." Previously married to actors Edward Norris and George Brent, from both of whom she was divorced, she wed actor Scott McKay in July, 1966. On January 21, 1967, she died of cancer at her San Fernando Valley home.

Ann Sheridan with Robert Cummings and Ronald Reagan in King's Row (Warner Bros., 1941).

Milburn Stone with Julie Bishop in Strange Conquest
(Universal, 1946).

Milburn Stone (1904–   )

Milburn Stone was born July 5, 1904, in Burrton, Kansas, and after graduation from high school there he was given a chance to attend the U.S. Naval Academy at Annapolis. He turned this opportunity down to try his hand at acting. He joined the Helen B. Ross Repertory Company and toured the Midwest. He joined other repertory companies during 1922 through 1932 with an occasional time out as a song and dance man in vaudeville. He also appeared in Sinclair Lewis' *The Jayhawker* on Broadway.

He moved to Hollywood and his first role was a small one in Paramount's *The Milky Way* in 1936 starring Harold Lloyd. He also appeared in *China Clipper, The Three Mesquiteers, Two in a Crowd,* and *Atlantic Flight.* In 1937 he was given his first starring role in *Federal Bullets* and co-starred in *Swing It—Professor* with Pinky Tomlin. In 1938 he was given the lead in *Port of Missing Girls.* In 1939 he co-starred with John Trent in four *Tailspin Tommy* episodes for Mon-

ogram, *Mystery Plane, Stunt Pilot, Sky Patrol,* and *Danger Flight.* He played the role of Skeeter.

He has many featured roles in films of all types for virtually every studio and many times played the villain and the "heavy" in many western films. He also starred in several serials. Some of his other films include *Crime School, King of the Turf, Young Mr. Lincoln, Colorado, Reap the Wild Wind, Sherlock Holmes Faces Death, The Frozen Ghost, Calamity Jane and Sam Bass, The Judge, Black Tuesday,* and *The Long Grey Line.*

He has obtained his greatest fame in television's "Gunsmoke" which began in 1955 and is still going strong. His portrayal as the cantankerous but lovable Doc earned him a well-deserved Emmy as Best Supporting Actor in 1968. The same year he had his first heart attack, he had another two years later and a third in 1971. He underwent successful open-heart surgery and rejoined "Gunsmoke" in 1972.

Lyle Talbot (1902–   )

Lyle Talbot was born Lisle Henderson, February 8, 1902, in Pittsburgh, Pennsylvania. His ancestors came from Ireland and Scotland. His mother's parents first settled in Pennsylvania around Pittsburgh and later migrated out west to Nebraska and Wyoming. His father's family settled in Nebraska and were pioneers and farmers. His father's name was Henderson. His grandmother's family in Ireland had the family name of Hollywood which is an old Irish name and a locale in Ireland. He took the name of Talbot when very young making it his legal name.

He started his acting career with his parents in traveling "Rep" and tent shows throughout the Midwest from Wisconsin to Colorado, *The Winninger Players, The Chase-Lister Co.,* etc. He then started playing in stock companies throughout the United States. He also had his own company *The Talbot Players* in Memphis.

He was signed by Warner Bros. in 1931 and his first film was *Love is a Racket* with Douglas Fairbanks, Jr., Lee Tracy, and Lila Lee. He had many leading and featured roles in a long film career and his films included *Three On A Match, No more Orchids, 20,000 Years in Sing Sing, One Night of Love, Oil For the Lamps of China, Man, Change of Heart, She's in the Army,* and many others. His favorite role was that of Bud in *20,000 Years in Sing Sing* with Spencer Tracy in 1933. He also appeared in several 15-episode serials including *The Atom Man versus Superman* for Columbia in 1950 in which he portrayed the lead villain, The Atom Man. He also appeared in many western films.

On television he appeared on the "Ozzie and Harriet Show" for 11 years and a long run with "Burns and Allen," "Bob Cummings," "The Lucy Show," and a hundred or more different shows.

Lyle Talbot in It Happened in New York *(Universal, 1935).*

He played on Broadway in *Separate Rooms,* which ran for two years, and a revival of *South Pacific* with Florence Henderson that was produced by Richard Rodgers at the Lincoln Center.

Although he appeared in over 150 movies, he has always preferred the theater and is still active in this medium as well as television.

Lee Tracy (1898–1968)

Lee Tracy was an actor whose machine-gun delivery typified the breezy spirit of the talkies when sound came to the movies. Born William Lee Tracy, he was the original Hildy Johnson in the 1928 *Front Page* of Charles MacArthur and Ben Hecht, and was thence forever typecast as the casting directors' idea of the ideal newspaperman. In the theater, film, and television, he frequently played a hard-bitten journalist. He soared to movie fame in the early 1930s with rapid-fire dialogue as a Broadway columnist loosely patterned after Walter Winchell in *Blessed Event*. His first screen role was the 1929 *Big Time*. Although born in Atlanta, Tracy, as the son of a railroader, lived in many parts of the South and Midwest. He was an officer in both World Wars I and II.

After the first war, he followed up some exposure in vaudeville and stock with a Broadway debut in 1924 in *The Show Off* and stardom, two years later, in *Broadway*. Possibly his best remembered nonnewspaper role was the Truman-like Arthur Hockstader in Gore Vidal's *The Best Man* in 1960. When he played the same role in the film version, it won him an Academy Award nomination.

His later years were devoted to television parts including his role as Martin Kane in "Martin Kane, Private Eye." On October 18, 1968, he died of cancer and left an estate valued at more than $2,000,000. In his will Tracy left all income to his wife and upon her death to a number of charities including the Motion Picture Relief Fund, the Midnight Mission, and the Salvation Army. The latter was included, he said shortly before his death, because, "they were the first

Lee Tracy with Gloria Stuart in **Wanted: Jean Turner** *(RKO, 1936).*

ones on the job in both world wars." Of the Midnight Mission, Tracy, who had done some heavy drinking during his lifetime, said that, "I couldn't leave that one out because there, but for the grace of God, go I."

Claire Trevor with George Raft in I Stole a Million
(Universal, 1939).

Claire Trevor (1912–   )

Claire Trevor was born Claire Wemlinger on March 8, 1912, in Bensonhurst, Long Island. Her family moved to Larchmont, New York, and she graduated from high school in Mamaroneck, New York. She attended Columbia University and the American Academy of Dramatic Arts. In 1929 she got her first part with a group of repertory players and traveled a great deal. Upon her return to New York she was signed by a Warner Bros. scout to do a series of shorts for that studio.

After her small taste of film making she returned to theater work and had Broadway performances in *Whistling in the Dark* in 1932 and *The Party's Over* in 1933. Twentieth Century-Fox offered her a screen contract that year and she accepted. Her first full-length screen appearance was in a George O'Brien western entitled *Life in the Raw* in 1933. She followed this performance with a second western also with O'Brien in the same year called *The Last Trail*.

Before the next half decade was over she was called "Queen of the 'B's'" as she appeared time and again in Fox films in this capacity. In 1937 she was given a small part in *Dead End* but she made the most of it as it allowed her to receive her first Oscar nomination for Best Supporting Actress. In 1937 she also appeared on radio for

CBS and for three years she portrayed Lorelei Kilbourne, society editor of the Illustrated Press, as Edward G. Robinson played the editor, Steve Wilson, in "Big Town."

During her career she appeared in many films including *Dante's Inferno, Human Cargo, Second Honeymoon, The Amazing Dr. Clitterhouse, Valley of the Giants, Stagecoach, Allegheny Uprising, Honky Tonk, Murder, My Sweet, Johnny Angel, Key Largo, The Lucky Stiff, My Man and I, The High and the Mighty, Lucy Gallant, Marjorie Morningstar, The Stripper,* and *How to Murder Your Wife.*

In 1939 she was given the choice role of Dallas opposite John Wayne in the classic *Stagecoach*. Although she was a success it did not further her career. In 1948 she was assigned the part of Gaye, Edward G. Robinson's mistress in *Key Largo* and her portrayal was so strong she won the Academy Award for Best Supporting Actress. Her third nomination came in 1954 for her role of May Holst in *The High and the Mighty*. In 1956 she won an Emmy for her TV performance in *Dodsworth*.

Three Academy nominations, one Oscar, one Emmy aren't too bad for the gal who was once labeled "Queen of the 'B's'."

Sonny Tufts (1912–1970)

Sonny Tufts was a Boston-born actor who played both cowboys and suave leading-man roles with equal verve. He was one of the few Boston Brahmins to become a movie actor. At the age of eight he decided that he would become a singer instead of following in the steps of his many ancestors who formed the pillars of Boston's merchant and banking communities.

To attain his goal, he joined his church choir and, after a year spent studying with operatic coaches, he won an audition with the Metropolitan Opera in New York. The audition won him a year's tuition for voice study. He attended Yale over the mild opposition of several Harvard relatives after he had studied trap drums at Philips-Exeter prep school. In college he organized dance bands and his musical aggregations played on a number of ship crossings of the Atlantic during summer months.

He found acting roles on Broadway in such shows as *Who's Who* and *Sing For Your Supper,* as well as occasional spots in night clubs including The Famous Door and The Beachcomber in New York and the White Hall at Palm Beach, Florida.

These engagements soon led him to Paramount Pictures, which signed him after his first screen test.

His first film was *So Proudly We Hail,* which started him on his way to success, starring opposite such actresses as Betty Hutton in *Cross My Heart* and *Too Good to Be True,* Veronica Lake in *Miss Susie Slagle's,* and with Bing Crosby in the musical, *Here Comes the Waves.* By the 1950s, he was cast in *The Seven Year Itch* with Marilyn Monroe, but by the end of the decade he had begun to ease out of films into retirement. Tuft's good looks and tall bearing made him a favorite with women audiences.

He drank rather heavily for a time and his wife, former dancer Barbara Dare, divorced him after fifteen years of marriage in 1953. He was arrested several times for drunkenness over the years, spent several years on a Texas ranch and finally returned to Hollywood, where he lived, and made occasional guest appearances on television until his death. On June 4, 1970, he died of pneumonia at St. John's Hospital in Santa Monica.

Sonny Tufts with Betty Hutton in Cross My Heart
(Paramount, 1946).

Lupe Velez (1909–1944)

Lupe Velez was known to moviegoers as the "Mexican Spitfire" because of her volcanic Latin temperament on the screen and off.

She was born on July 18, 1909, in San Luis Potosi, a suburb of Mexico City. Her mother was an opera singer and her father a colonel in the Mexican army. She was stage struck as a child and obtained her first role on the stage in *Rataplan*, a musical comedy, in Mexico City. Her first appearance in Hollywood was on the stage in *Music Box Revue* produced by Fanchon and Marco. She was signed to a contract by Hal Roach and appeared in several of his comedies. Her first role to attract wide attention was as the wild mountain girl in the Douglas Fairbanks picture, *The Gaucho,* produced in 1927. From that time she played top roles in all the major studios winding up her career with the Mexican Spitfire series at RKO.

She carried on many highly publicized off-screen romances and had a stormy marriage to Johnny Weissmuller from 1933 to 1938. Her films included *Lady of the Pavements, Cuban Love Song, Hollywood Party, Girl From Mexico, Mexican Spitfire, Mexican Spitfire's Blessed Event,* and her last film *Redhead From Manhattan.*

On December 14, 1944, she committed suicide at her home in Beverly Hills from an overdose of sleeping tablets. She left notes indicating that a frustrated romance had precipitated the act.

Lupe Velez in **The Girl From Mexico** *(RKO, 1939).*

Helen Walker with Dennis O'Keefe and William Bendix in **Abroad With Two Yanks** *(United Artists, 1944).*

Helen Walker (1920–1968)

Helen Walker appeared in a number of films in the 1940s in both dramatic and comedy roles. She was born in Worcester, Massachusetts, and after appearing in several eastern stock companies, she was given the lead opposite Alexander Knox in *Jason* on Broadway, with the result that she was given a contract by Paramount. She was made Alan Ladd's lead as "Cute Eyes" the USO worker in *Lucky Jordan* in 1942.

Miss Walker was involved in an automobile accident on New Year's Eve, 1946, while returning from Palm Springs. A soldier hitchhiker was killed in the accident and her career was never the same after that incident. Her own severe injuries, a highly-publicized insurance investigation, and several civil suits against her (of which she was absolved of all blame) hurt her career. Among her film credits were *The Good Fellows, Abroad With Two Yanks, The Man in Half-Moon Street, Brewster's Millions, Murder, He Says* (a minor comedy classic in which she gave her best screen performance), *Duffy's Tavern, Cluny Brown, People Are Funny, The Homestretch, Call Northside 777, My Dear Secretary, Impact, My True Story, Problem Girls,* and her last film, *The Big Combo,* in 1955.

In 1960 it was reported that she had lost everything in a house fire. Some of Miss Walker's Hollywood friends including Hugh O'Brian, Dinah Shore, Ruth Roman, and Vivian Blaine staged a benefit for her. On March 10, 1968, she died of cancer in Hollywood.

Robert Walker with Judy Garland in **The Clock** *(MGM, 1945).*

Robert Walker (1914–1951)

Robert Hudson Walker was born October 13, 1915, in Salt Lake City, Utah, where his father was a local newspaper editor. He started his dramatic career while studying at the Army and Navy Military Academy in San Diego.

After many lean years he moved to Tulsa, Oklahoma, and secured work at a local radio station. Jennifer Jones was a co-worker and became his first wife. His voice attracted the attention of Metro scouts and he was given a screen test and a part in his first film *Bataan* in 1943. He was plagued by severe emotional disturbances and they became so frequent that Jennifer Jones divorced him in 1945, shortly after she had won an Oscar for her work in *The Song of Bernadette*. She was awarded the custody of their two children, Robert Jr., and Michael. She later married David O. Selznick.

In 1948 he married Barbara Ford, daughter of screen director John Ford but the marriage was brief, ending for the same reason as the first. His nervous ailments and publicized alcoholic escapades caused him to enter the Menninger Clinic in Topeka, Kansas. After lengthy treatment he returned to Hollywood. After his work in *Bataan* he climbed to stardom with roles in *Madame Curie* and *See Here, Private Hargrove*. He also played top roles in *Since You Went Away, Thirty Seconds Over Tokyo, The Clock, Her Highness and the Bellboy, What Next, Corporal Hargrove?, The Sailor Takes a Wife, Till the Clouds Roll By, The Sea of Grass, The Beginning of the End, Song of Love, One Touch of Venus, Please Believe Me, The Skipper Surprised His Wife, Vengeance Valley,* and *Strangers On a Train,* in which many critics felt was his finest performance. His last film assignment was with Helen Hayes in *My Son John* at RKO.

He died August 27, 1951, after having a reaction to a sedative administered by his physician.

Warren William (1894–1948)

Warren William was born Warren William Krech in Aitkin, Minnesota, on December 2, 1894. His father was a newspaper publisher and hopeful for a journalism career for his son. Warren had other ideas and went to New York after high school and attended the Academy of Dramatic Arts. He served with the army in France during World War I and remained there for awhile after the war was over touring army camps with a theatrical troupe.

Upon returning to the states his first role on the stage was as a pickle salesman in *Mrs. Jimmie Thompson* in 1920. This was followed by a tour with a road company in *I Love You* and he then had the opportunity for his first Broadway appearances in the Rachel Crothers play *Expressing Willie*. He had established his popularity with Broadway audiences and in 1931 he appeared in his first film, *Expensive Women*. Other films in which he appeared were *Honor of the Family, Woman from Monte Carlo, The Match King, Three On A Match, Gold Diggers of 1933, Cleopatra, Widow from Monte Carlo, Stage Struck, Go West, Young Man, Madame X, Lillian Russell,* and *Passport to Suez.*

He gained his greatest fame playing detectives and D.A.'s. From 1939 through 1943 he portrayed *Michael Lanyard, the Lone Wolf* in eight films for Columbia. The premise for these films was that he was a reformed jewel robber who specialized in solving similar crimes. He also portrayed another sleuth, Philo Vance, in the *Dragon Murder Case* in 1934 and *The Gracie Allen Mur-*

Warren William with Gracie Allen in **The Gracie Allen Murder Case** *(Paramount, 1939).*

der Case in 1939.

He retired from films in 1947, but appeared on several radio programs. He died September 24, 1948, of multiple mycloma.

Grant Withers (1905–1959)

Grant Withers was born January 17, 1905, in Pueblo, Colorado. When his childhood turned to boyhood, his parents sent him to Kemper Military Academy in Boonville, Missouri, which was a fitting education for the son of the president of the Iron City Fuel Company. At Kemper he went in for plenty of swimming, fencing, and drilling. He also had a part in the school play entitled *Clarence*.

After graduation he moved to Los Angeles where he tried his hand as a salesman for the Standard Oil Company. He left this to work for the *Los Angeles Record* newspaper. He stayed there for a year and a half as a police reporter and covered the celebrated Bebe Daniels five-day stay in jail for speeding. He worked as an extra in a Douglas MacLean comedy, and his interest in newspaper work waned and he decided that he wanted to become a movie actor.

He met Fanchon Royer and she told him he'd go over big in pictures and suggested that she manage him. He worked in an Elinor Glyn picture at $100 a week. She managed to get him other openings and soon he had steady work. His work in *Hearts in Exile* in 1929 gained for him a five-year contract with Warner Brothers. He starred in such films as *Secrets of Wu Sin, Rip Roaring Riley, Paradise Express, Bill Cracks Down, Mr. Wong, Detective, Telephone Operator, Held For Ransom, Mr. Wong in Chinatown, Navy Secrets*, and *Daughter of the Tong*. He was featured in many other films and was equally at home in "heavy" roles. His films numbered well over one hundred.

He was also active in serials playing the lead in *The Fighting Marines* in 1935 for Mascot, and *Jungle Jim* and *Radio Patrol* both in 1937 for Universal. He was also featured in *Tailspin Tommy* for Universal in 1934 and *The Secret of Treasure Island* in 1938 for Columbia.

He hit the headlines in 1929 when he eloped to Yuma, Arizona, with seventeen-year-old Loretta Young. Her mother met the plane as they arrived back and annulment proceedings were started. They were divorced in 1931.

In his later years his acting roles were reduced to heavies, character, and bit parts in westerns. He had been married five times and was in financial straits.

On March 28, 1959, his landlord discovered his body propped up in bed, wearing glasses, his left hand clutching the telephone receiver with a novel open before him. He had been dead about 24 hours, the victim of an overdose of sleeping tablets.

Grant Withers with Keith Richards in Duke of Chicago *(Republic, 1949).*

Fay Wray (1907–   )

Fay Wray is most famous as the actress in the clutches of the mighty King Kong as he stood atop the Empire State Building. She was born on her father's ranch on September 10, 1907, in Alberta, Canada. As a child she moved to Los Angeles. She was cast as a teenager in Erich von Stroheim's lavish 1926 film, *The Wedding March.* She became a star after that picture was released in 1928.

Throughout her film career she appeared opposite some of the most famous male stars such as Gary Cooper, Richard Arlen, Ronald Colman, Fredric March, and Spencer Tracy. Some of her more than 100 films include *The Texan, The Sea God, Dirigible, Doctor X, King Kong, The Big Brain, Viva Villa!, Woman in the Dark, Navy Secrets,* and *Not a Ladies' Man.* In 1942 she retired after she married Hollywood scenarist Robert Riskin, who wrote *It Happened One Night.* She was widowed in 1955 and thereafter reactivated her career in television and in several films. She now lives in the Brentwood section of Los Angeles.

Fay Wray in King Kong *(RKO, 1933).*

3
Star Gallery

Julie Adams: October 17, 1928 (Waterloo, Iowa)–

John Agar: January 13, 1921 (Chicago, Illinois)–

Brian Aherne: May 2, 1902 (Worcestershire, England)–

Eddie Albert: April 22, 1908 (Rock Island, Illinois)–

Frank Albertson: February 2, 1909 (Fergus Falls, Minnesota)–February 29, 1964

Hardie Albright: December 16, 1905 (Charleroi, Pennsylvania)–

Lola Albright: July 20, 1925 (Akron, Ohio)–

Ross Alexander: July 27, 1907 (New York, New York)–
January 2, 1937

Louise Allbritton: July 3, 1920 (Oklahoma City, Oklahoma)–

Bob Allen: March 28, 1906 (Mt. Vernon, New York)–

Astrid Allwyn: November 27, 1910 (South Manchester, Connecticut)–

117

Adrienne Ames: August 3, 1908 (Ft. Worth, Texas)–
May 31, 1947

Merry Anders: May 22, 1934 (Chicago, Illinois)–

118

Mary Anderson: April 3, 1924 (Birmingham, Alabama)–

Keith Andes: July 12, 1920 (Ocean City, New Jersey)–

Heather Angel: February 1, 1909 (Oxford, England)–

Annabella: July 14, 1912 (Paris, France)–

John Archer: May 8, 1915 (Osceola, Nebraska)–

Eve Arden: April 30, 1912 (Mill Valley, California)-

121

Richard Arlen: September 1, 1900 (Charlottesville, Virginia)–

Robert Armstrong: November 20, 1896 (Saginaw, Michigan)–April 20, 1973

Jean Arthur: October 17, 1905 (New York, New York)–

Lew Ayres: December 28, 1908 (Minneapolis Minnesota)–

Lauren Bacall: September 16, 1924 (New York, New York)–

Diane Baker: February 25, 1938 (Hollywood, California)–

Anne Bancroft: September 17, 1931 (Bronx, New York)–

Lynn Bari: December 18, 1915 (Roanoke, Virginia)–

Lex Barker: May 8, 1919 (Rye, New York)— May 11, 1973

Binnie Barnes: March 25, 1905 (London, England)–

Mona Barrie: December 18, 1909 (London, England)–

Wendy Barrie: April 18, 1913 (Hong Kong, China)–

127

Gene Barry: June 14, 1921 (New York, New York)–

Anne Baxter: May 7, 1923 (Michigan City, Indiana)–

128

Warner Baxter: March 29, 1889 (Columbus, Ohio)–
May 7, 1951

John Beal: August 13, 1909 (Joplin, Missouri)–

129

Ralph Bellamy: June 17, 1904 (Chicago, Illinois)–

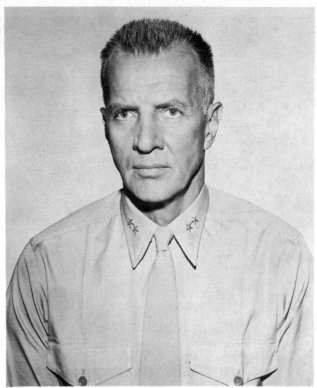

Bruce Bennett: May 19, 1909 (Tacoma, Washington)–

Turhan Bey: March 30, 1919 (Vienna, Austria)–

Julie Bishop: August 30, 1917 (Denver, Colorado)–

Janet Blair: April 23, 1921 (Altoona, Pennsylvania)–

Mari Blanchard: April 13, 1927 (Long Beach, California)–May 10, 1970

Ann Blyth: August 16, 1928 (Mt. Kisco, New York)–

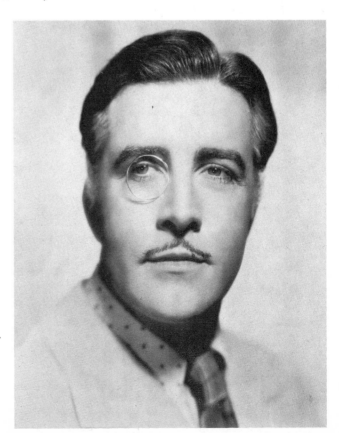

John Boles: October 27, 1895 (Greenville, Texas)–
February 27, 1969

Dorris Bowdon: December 23, 1916 (Coldwater, Mississippi)–

Karin Booth: June 19, – (Minneapolis, Minnesota)–

134

Lee Bowman: December 28, 1914 (Cincinnati, Ohio)–

William Boyd: June 5, 1895 (Cambridge, Ohio)–
September 12, 1972

Grace Bradley: September 21, 1913 (Brooklyn, New York)–

Olympe Bradna: August 12, 1920 (Paris, France)–

Scott Brady: September 13, 1924 (Brooklyn, New York)–

George Brent: March 15, 1904 (Dublin, Ireland)–

David Brian: August 5, 1914 (New York, New York)–

Mary Brian: February 17, 1908 (Dallas, Texas)–

Lloyd Bridges: January 15, 1913 (San Leandro, California)–

Barbara Britton: September 26, 1923 (Long Beach, California)–

Clive Brook: June 1, 1891 (London, England)–

Hillary Brooke: September 6, – (Long Island, New York)–

140

Geraldine Brooks: October 29, 1925 (New York, New York)–

Phyllis Brooks: July 18, 1914 (Boise, Idaho)–

141

David Bruce: January 6, 1914 (Kankakee, Illinois)–

Tom Brown: January 6, 1913 (New York, New York)–

Virginia Bruce: September 29, 1910 (Minneapolis, Minnesota)–

Ralph Byrd: April 22, 1909 (Dayton, Ohio)– August 18, 1952

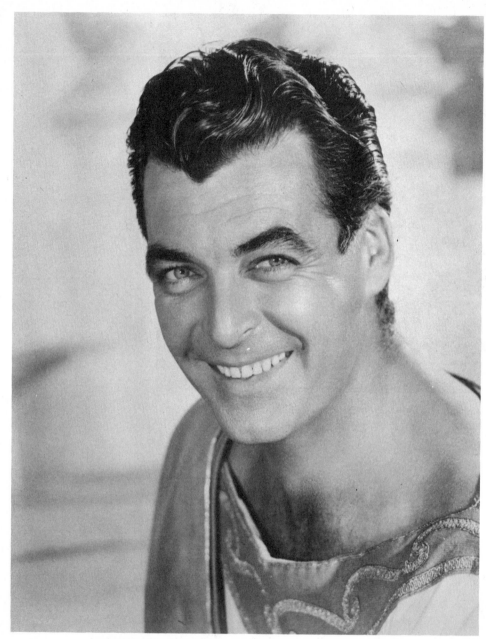

Rory Calhoun: August 8, 1923 (Los Angeles, California)–

Corinne Calvet: April 30, 1921 (Paris, France)–

Rod Cameron: December 7, 1912 (Calgary, Alberta, Canada)–

MacDonald Carey: March 15, 1913 (Sioux City, Iowa)–

Phil Carey: July 15, 1925 (Hackensack, New Jersey)–

Mary Carlisle: February 3, 1912 (Boston, Massachusetts)—

Richard Carlson: April 29, 1912 (Albert Lee, Minnesota)—

Leslie Caron: July 1, 1931 (Paris, France)–

Madeleine Carroll: February 26, 1906 (W. Bromwich, England)–

Helena Carter: August 24, 1923 (New York, New York)–

Janis Carter: October 10, 1917 (Cleveland, Ohio)–

Lynne Carver: September 13, 1909 (Lexington, Kentucky)–August 12, 1955

Joan Caulfield: June 1, 1922 (Orange, New Jersey)–

Helen Chandler: February 1, 1906 (Charleston, South Carolina)–April 30, 1965

Jeff Chandler: December 15, 1918 (Brooklyn, New York)–June 17, 1961

Marguerite Chapman: March 9, 1920 (Chatham, New York)–

Dane Clark: February 18, 1915 (New York, New York)–

Cyd Charrise: March 8, 1921 (Amarillo, Texas)–

Mae Clarke: August 16, 1910 (Philadelphia, Pennsylvania)–

Montgomery Clift: October 17, 1920 (Omaha, Ne-braska)–July 23, 1966

June Clyde: December 2, 1909 (St. Joseph, Missouri)–

154

Steve Cochran: May 25, 1917 (Eureka, California)–
June 15, 1965

Joan Collins: May 23, 1933 (London, England)–

Richard Conte: March 24, 1914 (New York, New York)–

Donald Cook: September 26, 1901 (Portland, Oregon)–October 1, 1961

156

Jackie Cooper: September 15, 1921 (Los Angeles, California)–

Wendell Corey: March 20, 1914 (Dracut, Massachusetts)–November 8, 1968

Ricardo Cortez: September 19, 1899 (Brooklyn, New York)–

Dolores Costello: September 17, 1905 (Pittsburgh, Pennsylvania)–

James Craig: February 4, 1912 (Nashville, Tennessee)–

Jeanne Crain: May 25, 1925 (Barstow, California)–

Broderick Crawford: December 9, 1911 (Philadelphia, Pennsylvania)–

Bob Cummings: June 9, 1910 (Joplin, Missouri)–

Arlene Dahl: August 11, 1924 (Minneapolis, Minnesota)–

Dan Dailey: December 14, 1914 (New York, New York)–

Lili Damita: September 10, 1907 (Paris, France)–

Helmut Dantine: October 7, 1918 (Vienna, Austria)–

Danielle Darrieux: May 1, 1917 (Bordeaux, France)–

Nancy Davis: July 6, 1922 (New York, New York)–

Laraine Day: October 13, 1917 (Roosevelt, Utah)–

Yvonne DeCarlo: September 1, 1922 (Vancouver, Canada)–

Gloria DeHaven: July 23, 1924 (Los Angeles, California)–

Myrna Dell: March 5, 1924 (Los Angeles, California)–

Katherine DeMille: June 20, 1915 (Vancouver, British Columbia)–

Richard Denning: March 27, 1914 (Poughkeepsie, New York)–

164

Reginald Denny: November 20, 1891 (Richmond, Surrey, England)–June 17, 1967

John Derek: August 12, 1926 (Hollywood, California)–

Richard Dix: July 18, 1893 (St. Paul, Minnesota)–
September 20, 1949

Claire Dodd: December 29, 1908 (New York, New York)– November 23, 1973

Faith Domergue: June 16, 1925 (New Orleans, Louisiana)–

166

Jeff Donnell: July 10, 1921 (South Windham, Maine)–

Johnny Downs: October 10, 1915 (Brooklyn, New York)–

Charles Drake: October 2, 1914 (New York, New York)–

Tom Drake: August 5, 1918 (New York, New York)–

Ellen Drew: November 23, 1915 (Kansas City, Missouri)–

Joanne Dru: January 31, 1923 (Logan, West Virginia)–

Howard Duff: November 24, 1917 (Bremerton, Washington)–

Dixie Dunbar: January 19, 1919 (Montgomery, Alabama)–

Stephen Dunne: January 13, 1918 (Northampton, Massachusetts)–

Deanna Durbin: December 4, 1921 (Winnipeg, Canada)–

Barbara Eden: August 23, 1934 (Tucson, Arizona)–

Richard Egan: July 29, 1923 (San Francisco, California)–

Sally Eilers: December 11, 1908 (New York, New York)–

Bill Elliott: October 16, 1905 (Pattonsburg, Missouri)–
November 27, 1965

Leif Erickson: October 27, 1914 (Alameda, Califor-
nia)–

Dale Evans: October 31, 1912 (Uvalde, Texas)–

Joan Evans: July 18, 1934 (New York, New York)–

Madge Evans: July 1, 1909 (New York, New York)–

Jinx Falkenburg: January 21, 1919 (Barcelona, Spain)–

William Eythe: April 7, 1918 (Mars, Pennsylvania)–
January 26, 1957

Mel Ferrer: August 25, 1917 (Elberson, New Jersey)–

Betty Field: February 8, 1918 (Boston, Massachusetts)–September 13, 1973

Virginia Field: November 4, 1917 (London, England)—

Rhonda Fleming: August 10, 1923 (Los Angeles, California)—

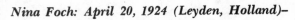
Nina Foch: April 20, 1924 (Leyden, Holland)–

Wallace Ford: February 12, 1898 (Batton, Lanca-shire, England)–June 11, 1966

Norman Foster: December 13, 1900 (Richmond, Indiana)–

Anne Francis: September 16, 1930 (Ossinging, New York)–

Arthur Franz: February 29, 1920 (Perth Amboy, New Jersey)–

Jane Frazee: July 18, 1920 (Duluth, Minnesota)–

Mona Freeman: June 9, 1926 (Baltimore, Maryland)-

Betty Furness: January 3, 1916 (New York, New York)-

Franciska Gaal: February 1, 1904 (Budapest, Hungary)—

Zsa Zsa Gabor: February 6, 1923 (Budapest, Hungary)—

William Gargan: July 17, 1905 (Brooklyn, New York)–

Beverly Garland: October 17, 1930 (Santa Cruz, California)–

Mitzi Gaynor: September 4, 1930 (Chicago, Illinois)–

Gladys George: September 13, 1900 (Hatton, Maine)–
December 8, 1954

Wynne Gibson: July 3, 1907 (New York, New York)–

Frances Gifford: December 7, 1922 (Long Beach, California)–

Gloria Grahame: November 28, 1925 (Los Angeles, California)—

Farley Granger: July 1, 1925 (San Jose, California)—

Stewart Granger: May 6, 1913 (London, England)–

Bonita Granville: February 2, 1923 (New York, New York)–

Coleen Gray: October 23, 1922 (Staplehurst, Nebraska)–

Kathryn Grayson: February 9, 1922 (Winston Salem, North Carolina)–

Richard Greene: August 24, 1914 (Plymouth, England)–

Nan Grey: July 25, 1918 (Houston, Texas)–

Virginia Grey: March 22, 1916 (Hollywood, California)–

Sigrid Gurie: May 18, 1915 (Brooklyn, New York)–
August 14, 1969

Anne Gwynne: December 10, 1918 (Waco, Texas)–

Reed Hadley: June 25, 1911 (Petrolia, Texas)–

Jean Hagen: August 3, 1925 (Chicago, Illinois)–

Barbara Hale: April 18, 1922 (DeKalb, Illinois)–

Jack Haley: August 10, 1902 (Boston, Massachusetts)–

Jon Hall: February 26, 1913 (Fresno, California)–

Neil Hamilton: September 9, 1899 (Lynn, Massachu-setts)–

*Russell Hardie: May 20, 1906 (Buffalo, New York)–
July 21, 1973*

Ann Harding: August 7, 1901 (San Antonio, Texas)–

Dolores Hart: October 20, 1939 (Chicago, Illinois)–

191

Richard Hart: April 14, 1915 (Providence, Rhode Island)–January 2, 1951

June Haver: June 10, 1926 (Rock Island, Illinois)–

June Havoc: November 8, 1916 (Seattle, Washington)–

Sterling Hayden: March 26, 1916 (Montclair, New Jersey)–

Louis Hayward: March 19, 1909 (Johannesburg, South Africa)–

Wanda Hendrix: November 3, 1928 (Jacksonville, Florida)–

William Henry: November 19, 1906 (Los Angeles, California)–

Gloria Holden: September 5, 1911 (London, England)–

Celeste Holm: April 29, 1919 (New York, New York)–

Miriam Hopkins: October 18, 1902 (Bainbridge, Georgia)–October 9, 1972

John Howard: April 14, 1913 (Cleveland, Ohio)–

John Hubbard: April 23, 1914 (East Chicago, Indiana)–

Warren Hull: January 17, 1903 (Niagara Falls, New York)–

197

Marsha Hunt: October 17, 1917 (Chicago, Illinois)–

Ian Hunter: June 13, 1900 (Cape Town, South Africa)–

Jeffrey Hunter: November 25, 1925 (New Orleans, Louisiana)–May 27, 1969

Kim Hunter: November 12, 1922 (Detroit, Michigan)–

Ruth Hussey: October 30, 1914 (Providence, Rhode Island)–

Josephine Hutchinson: October 12, 1909 (Seattle, Washington)–

Robert Hutton: July 11, 1920 (Kingston, New York)–

Betty Hutton: February 26, 1921 (Battle Creek, Michigan)–

Martha Hyer: August 10, 1924 (Ft. Worth, Texas)–

Leila Hyams: May 1, 1905 (New York, New York)–

201

John Ireland: January 30, 1914 (Vancouver, British Columbia)–

Dean Jagger: November 7, 1903 (Lima, Ohio)–

Gloria Jean: April 14, 1928 (Buffalo, New York)–

Adele Jergens: November 26, 1922 (Brooklyn, New York)–

Glynis Johns: October 5, 1923 (Durban, South Africa)–

Allan Jones: October 14, 1905 (Scranton, Pennsylvania)–

Carolyn Jones: April 28, 1929 (Amarillo, Texas)–

Jennifer Jones: March 2, 1919 (Tulsa, Oklahoma)–

Shirley Jones: March 31, 1933 (Smithton, Pennsylvania)–

Louis Jourdan: June 19, 1921 (Marseille, France)–

Brenda Joyce: February 26, 1916 (Kansas City, Missouri)–

206

Arline Judge: February 21, 1912 (Bridgeport, Connecticut)–

Howard Keel: April 13, 1917 (Gillespie, Illinois)–

Brian Keith: November 14, 1921 (Bayonne, New Jersey)—

Arthur Kennedy: February 17, 1914 (Worcester, Massachusetts)—

Barbara Kent: December 16, 1908 (Gadsby, Canada)–

Deborah Kerr: September 30, 1921 (Helensburgh, Scotland)–

Evelyn Keyes: November 20, 1919 (Port Arthur, Texas)–

Evelyn Knapp: July 17, 1908 (Kansas City, Missouri)–

Elyse Knox: December 14, 1917 (Hartford, Connecticut)–

Alexander Knox: January 16, 1907 (Strathboy, Ontario, Canada)–

Arthur Lake: April 17, 1905 (Corbin, Kentucky)–

Elissa Landi: December 6, 1904 (Venice, Italy)–October 21, 1948

Rosemary Lane: April 14, 1916 (Indianola, Iowa)–

212

June Lang: May 5, 1915 (Minneapolis, Minnesota)–

Angela Lansbury: October 16, 1925 (London, England)–

Piper Laurie: January 22, 1932 (Detroit, Michigan)–

Peter Lawford: September 7, 1923 (London, England)–

Francis Lederer: November 6, 1906 (Prague, Karlin, Czech.)–

Anna Lee: January 3, 1914 (England)–

Joan Leslie: January 26, 1925 (Detroit, Michigan)–

Margaret Lindsay: September 19, 1910 (Dubuque, Iowa)–

Robert Livingston: December 8, 1908 (Quincy, Illinois)–

John Loder: January 8, 1898 (London, England)–

Audrey Long: April 14, 1924 (Orlando, Florida)–

Robert Lowery: October 17, 1916 (Kansas City, Missouri)–December 26, 1971

John Lund: February 6, 1913 (Rochester, New York)–

William Lundigan: June 12, 1914 (Syracuse, New York)–

218

Ida Lupino: February 4, 1914 (London, England)–

James Lydon: May 30, 1923 (Harrington Park, New Jersey)–

Jeffrey Lynn: February 16, 1909 (Auburn, Massachusetts)–

Helen Mack: November 13, 1913 (Rock Island, Illinois)–

Guy Madison: January 19, 1922 (Bakersfield, California)–

Dorothy Malone: January 30, 1925 (Chicago, Illinois)—

221

Adele Mara: April 28, 1923 (Highland Park, Michigan)—

Joan Marsh: July 10, 1915 (Portersville, California)–

Alan Marshal: January 20, 1909 (Sydney, Australia)–

Brenda Marshall: September 29, 1915 (Island of Ne-
groes, P.I.)–

222

Trudy Marshall: February 14, 1922 (Brooklyn, New York)–

James Mason: May 15, 1909 (Hudersfield, England)–

Ilona Massey: July 15, 1910 (Budapest, Hungary)–

Virginia Mayo: November 30, 1920 (St. Louis, Missouri)–

Dorothy McGuire: June 14, 1918 (Omaha, Nebraska)–

Stephen McNally: July 29, 1916 (New York, New York)–

Patricia Medina: July 19, 1923 (London, England)–

225 Una Merkel: December 10, 1903 (Covington, Kentucky)–

Burgess Meredith: November 16, 1908 (Cleveland, Ohio)–

Gertrude Michael: June 1, 1911 (Talladega, Alabama)–January 1, 1965

226

Vera Miles: August 23, 1930 (Boise City, Idaho)–

Isa Miranda: July 5, 1917 (Milan, Italy)–

227

Cameron Mitchell: November 4, 1918 (Dallastown, Pennsylvania)–

Ricardo Montalban: November 25, 1920 (Mexico City, Mexico)–

George Montgomery: August 29, 1916 (Brady, Montana)–

228

Robert Montgomery: May 21, 1904 (Beacon, New York)–

Cleo Moore: October 31, 1930 (Baton Rouge, Louisiana)– October 25, 1973

Constance Moore: January 18, 1922 (Sioux City, Iowa)—

Terry Moore: January 7, 1929 (Los Angeles, California)—

Patricia Morison: March 19, 1915 (New York, New York)—

Karen Morley: December 12, 1905 (Ottumwa, Iowa)–

Audie Murphy: June 20, 1924 (Kingston, Texas)–
May 28, 1971

George Murphy: July 4, 1902 (New Haven, Connecticut)–

George Nader: October 19, 1921 (Pasadena, California)–

Anne Nagel: September 30, 1915 (Boston, Massachusetts)–July 6, 1966 232

Conrad Nagel: March 16, 1897 (Keokuk, Iowa)–February 24, 1970

Patricia Neal: January 20, 1926 (Packard, Kentucky)–

Barry Nelson: April 16, 1925 (Oakland, California)–

Gene Nelson: March 24, 1920 (Seattle, Washington)–

234

Lori Nelson: August 15, 1933 (Santa Fe, New Mexico)–

Richard Ney: November 12, 1913 (New York, New York)–

Alex Nicol: January 20, 1919 (Ossining, New York)–

Marian Nixon: October 20, 1904 (Superior, Wisconsin)–

Edward Norris: March 10, 1911 (Philadelphia, Pennsylvania)–

Merle Oberon: February 19, 1911 (Tasmania, Australia)–

236

Dave O'Brien: May 31, 1912 (Big Springs, Texas)–
November 8, 1969

Edmond O'Brien: September 10, 1915 (New York,
New York)–

Pat O'Brien: November 11, 1899 (Milwaukee, Wisconsin)–

Donald O'Connor: August 30, 1925 (Chicago, Illinois)–

Martha O'Driscoll: March 4, 1922 (Tulsa, Oklahoma)–

Maureen O'Hara: August 17, 1920 (Dublin, Ireland)–

Dan O'Herlihy: May 1, 1919 (Wexford, Ireland)–

Warner Oland: October 3, 1880 (Ulmea, Sweden)–
August 6, 1938

239

Vivienne Osborne: December 10, 1910 (Des Moines, Iowa)–June 10, 1961

Michael O'Shea: March 17, 1906 (Hartford, Connecticut)– December 4, 1973

Maureen O'Sullivan: May 17, 1911 (County Roscommon, Ireland)–

Anita Page: August 4, 1910 (Flushing, New York)–

241

Gale Page: July 23, 1912 (Spokane, Washington)–

Janis Paige: September 16, 1922 (Tacoma, Washington)–

Robert Paige: December 2, 1910 (Indianapolis, Indiana)–

Debra Paget: August 19, 1933 (Denver, Colorado)–

Willard Parker: February 5, 1912 (New York, New York)–

Larry Parks: December 13, 1914 (Olathe, Kansas)–

Helen Parrish: March 12, 1922 (Columbus, Georgia)–
February 22, 1959

Gail Patrick: June 20, 1911 (Birmingham, Alabama)–

John Payne: May 23, 1912 (Roanoke, Virginia)–

Jean Peters: October 15, 1926 (Canton, Ohio)—

Walter Pidgeon: September 23, 1897 (East St. John, New Brunswick, Canada)—

Eleanor Powell: November 21, 1910 (Springfield, Massachusetts)—

246

Jane Powell: April 1, 1929 (Portland, Oregon)–

Robert Preston: June 8, 1918 (Newton Highlands, Massachusetts)–

Vincent Price: May 27, 1911 (St. Louis, Missouri)–

Roger Pryor: August 27, 1903 (New York, New York)–

Dick Purcell: August 6, 1905 (Greenwich, Connecticut)–April 11, 1944

Ella Raines: August 6, 1921 (Snoqualmie Falls, Washington)–

Vera Ralston: July 12, 1921 (Prague, Czech.)–

Aldo Ray: September 25, 1926 (Pen Argyl, Pennsylvania)–

Gene Raymond: August 13, 1908 (New York, New York)–

Paula Raymond: November 23, 1924 (San Francisco, California)–

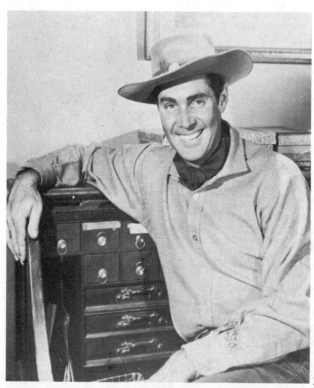

250

Philip Reed: March 25, 1908 (New York, New York)–

George Reeves: January 6, 1914 (Woodstock, Iowa)–
June 16, 1959

Michael Rennie: August 25, 1909 (Bradford, York-
shire, England)–June 10, 1971

*Craig Reynolds: July 15, 1907 (Anaheim, California)–
October 22, 1949*

Marjorie Reynolds: August 12, 1921 (Buhl, Idaho)–

Florence Rice: February 14, 1911 (Cleveland, Ohio)–

Beverly Roberts: May 19, 1914 (New York, New York)–

Lynne Roberts: November 22, 1919 (El Paso, Texas)–

Cliff Robertson: September 9, 1925 (La Jolla, California)—

Jean Rogers: March 25, 1916 (Belmont, Massachusetts)—

Gilbert Roland: December 11, 1905 (Chihuahua, Mexico)–

Ruth Roman: December 22, 1924 (Boston, Massachusetts)–

255

Shirley Ross: January 7, 1915 (Omaha, Nebraska)—

Jane Russell: June 21, 1921 (Bemidji, Minnesota)—

Ann Rutherford: November 2, 1917 (Toronto, Canada)–

Peggy Ryan: August 28, 1924 (Long Beach, California)–

Sheila Ryan: July 8, 1921 (Columbia, South Carolina)–

George Sanders: July 3, 1906 (St. Petersburg, Russia)–
April 25, 1972

Ann Savage: February 19, 1921 (Columbia, South Carolina)–

Martha Scott: September 22, 1914 (Jamesport, Missouri)–

Randolph Scott: January 23, 1903 (Orange County, Virginia)–

Dorothy Sebastian: April 26, 1905 (Birmingham, Alabama)–April 8, 1957

Anne Shirley: April 17, 1918 (New York, New York)–

Jean Simmons: January 31, 1929 (London, England)–

Simone Simon: April 23, 1914 (Marseille, France)—

Penny Singleton: September 15, 1908 (Philadelphia, Pennsylvania)—

Alexis Smith: June 8, 1921 (Penticton, Canada)—

Ann Sothern: January 22, 1909 (Valley City, North Dakota)–

Robert Stack: January 13, 1919 (Los Angeles, California)–

Charles Starrett: March 28, 1903 (Athol, Massachusetts)–

Anna Sten: December 3, 1908 (Kiev, Russia)–

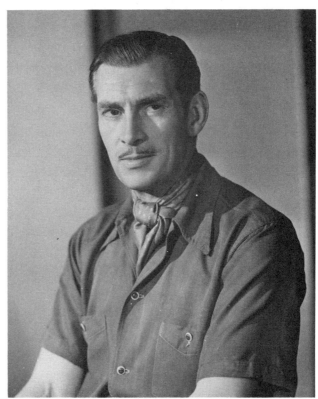

James Stephenson: April 14, 1889 (Selby, Yorkshire, England)–July 29, 1941

Jan Sterling: April 3, 1923 (New York, New York)-

Craig Stevens: July 8, 1918 (Liberty, Missouri)-

264

Mark Stevens: December 13, 1922 (Cleveland, Ohio)-

Gale Storm: April 5, 1922 (Bloomington, Texas)–

Gloria Stuart: July 14, 1911 (Santa Monica, California)–

Barry Sullivan: August 29, 1912 (New York, New York)–

John Sutton: October 22, 1908 (Rawalpindi, India)– July 10, 1963

Sylvia Sidney: August 8, 1910 (New York, New York)–

Lilyan Tashman: October 23, 1899 (New York, New York)–March 21, 1934)

Kent Taylor: May 11, 1907 (Nashua, Iowa)–

Don Terry: August 8, 1902 (Natick, Massachusetts)–

Philip Terry: March 7, 1909 (San Francisco, California)–

Ruth Terry: October 21, 1920 (Benton Harbor, Michigan)–

Phyllis Thaxter: November 29, 1920 (Portland, Maine)–

Genevieve Tobin: November 29, 1901 (New York, New York)—

Richard Todd: July 11, 1919 (Dublin, Eire)—

Thelma Todd: July 29, 1905 (Lawrence, Massachusetts)—December 16, 1935

Sidney Toler: April 28, 1874 (Warrensburg, Missouri)–February 12, 1947

Marta Toren: May 21, 1926 (Stockholm, Sweden)–February 19, 1957

Audrey Totter: December 20, 1918 (Joliet, Illinois)–

June Travis: August 7, 1914 (Chicago, Illinois)–

Forrest Tucker: February 12, 1915 (Plainsfield, Indiana)–

272

*Helen Twelvetrees: December 25, 1908 (Brooklyn,
New York)–February 13, 1958*

*Tom Tyler: August 9, 1903 (New York, New York)–
May 1, 1954*

Rudy Vallee: July 28, 1901 (Island Pond, Vermont)–

Evelyn Venable: October 18, 1913 (Cincinnati, Ohio)–

Vera Ellen: February 16, 1926 (Cincinnati, Ohio)–

Elena Verdugo: April 20, 1925 (Beaumont, Texas)–

Helen Vinson: September 17, 1908 (Beaumont, Texas)–

Theodore Von Eltz: November 5, 1893 (New Haven, Connecticut)–October 6, 1964

Jean Wallace: October 12, 1923 (Chicago, Illinois)–

Ruth Warrick: July 29, 1915 (St. Louis, Missouri)–

David Wayne: January 30, 1916 (Travers City, Michigan)–

Marjorie Weaver: March 2, 1913 (Grossville, Tennessee)–

Michael Whalen: June 30, 1908 (Wilkes-Barre, Pennsylvania)–

Arleen Whelan: September 16, 1916 (Salt Lake City, Utah)–

Robert Wilcox: May 19, 1910 (Rochester, New York)–
June 11, 1955

Henry Wilcoxon: September 8, 1905 (British West Indies)–

Cornel Wilde: October 13, 1915 (New York, New York)–

Bill Williams: May 21, 1916 (Brooklyn, New York)–

Dorothy Wilson: November 14, 1909 (Minneapolis, Minnesota)–

Marie Wilson: August 19, 1916 (Anaheim, California)–November 23, 1972

Marie Windsor: December 11, 1922 (Marysvale, Utah)–

Jane Withers: April 12, 1926 (Atlanta, Georgia)–

Joan Woodbury: December 17, 1915 (Los Angeles, California)–

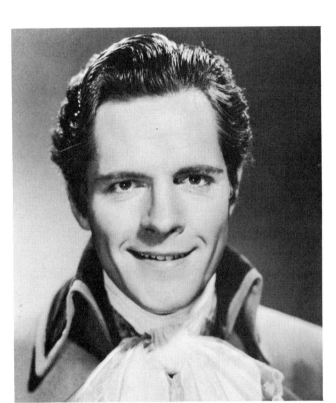

Donald Woods: December 2, 1906 (Brandon, Canada)–

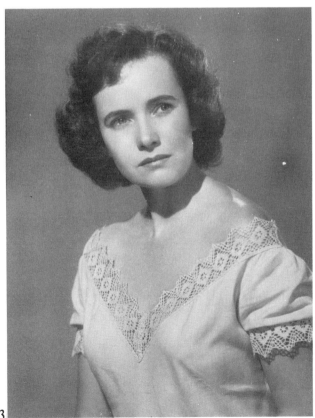

283

Teresa Wright: October 27, 1918 (New York, New York)–

Jane Wyatt: August 10, 1911 (Campgaw, New Jersey)—

May Wynn: January 8, 1930 (New York, New York)—

284

Gig Young: November 4, 1917 (St. Cloud, Minnesota)–

Vera Zorina: February 1, 1917 (Berlin, Germany)–